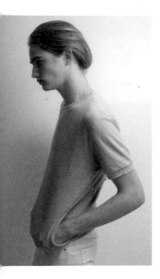

MODERN
MENSWEAR

HYWEL DAVIES

LAURENCE KING

Published in 2009 by
Laurence King Publishing Ltd
361–373 City Road
London EC1V 1LR
United Kingdom
Tel: +44 20 7841 6900
Fax: +44 20 7841 6910
e-mail: enquiries@laurenceking.com
www.laurenceking.com

A catalogue record for this book is available from the British Library.

ISBN 13: 978-1-85669-595-4

Printed in China

Design: Byboth

On the jacket: Duckie Brown, Fall/Winter 08. Photography Platon.

PAGE 1: MAISON MARTIN MARGIELA, AUTUMN/WINTER 06/07.
PAGE 2: WOODS & WOODS, AUTUMN/WINTER 06/07.
PAGE 3: BLAAK, SPRING/SUMMER 07.
PAGE 4: WALTER VAN BEIRENDONCK, AUTUMN/WINTER 96/97.
PAGE 5: FRANK LEDER, AUTUMN/WINTER 04/05.

CONTENTS

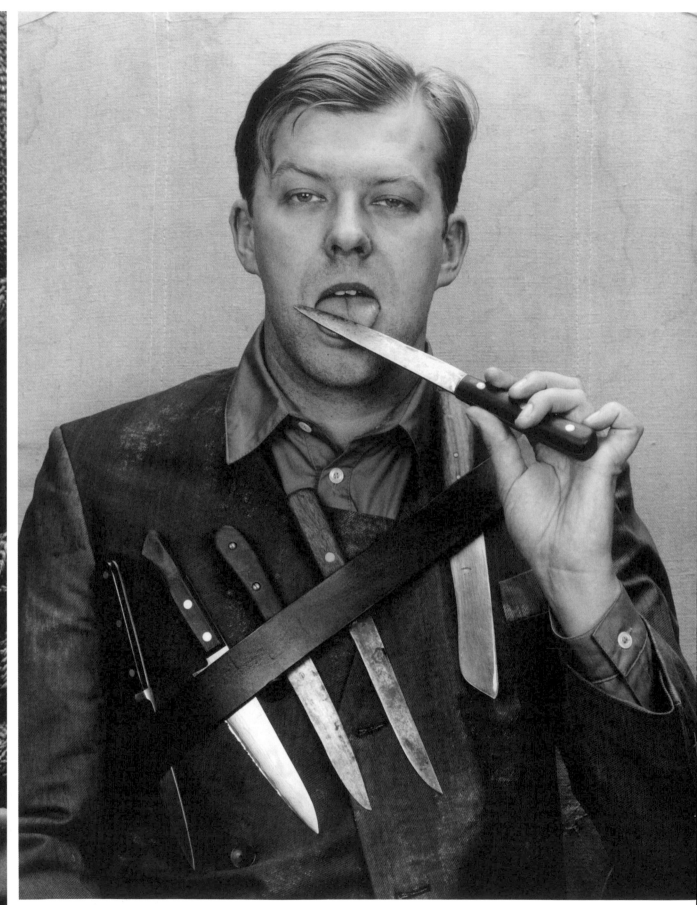

ABOVE: FRANK LEDER, 2005. *OPPOSITE, LEFT:* COSMIC WONDER
LIGHT SOURCE, SPRING/SUMMER 07. *OPPOSITE, RIGHT:* SPASTOR,
AUTUMN/WINTER 05/06.

INTRODUCTION

MODERN MENSWEAR is primarily concerned with COMMUNICATING INDIVIDUALITY. A shift in attitude has encouraged the male consumer to undertake extreme measures to AVOID CONFORMITY. Following the rule book is not the prescribed method in being stylish. CONTEMPORARY MENSWEAR PROVIDES MEN WITH THE OPPORTUNITY TO EXPRESS THEIR INDIVIDUALITY AND THIS IS NOW THE GREATEST LUXURY AVAILABLE.

By escaping uniformity male consumers now have an immense variety of clothing to choose from. Providing this variety is a wealth of talented visionary designers offering contemporary options in clothing and its associated products.

Specific groups no longer appropriate generic garments, as contemporary menswear is challenging, diverse and exciting. Although once the shirt and tie represented the businessman and jeans and T-shirts stood for youth and rebellion, now anybody can decide to wear anything. Menswear commentators no longer deliberate over whether a three-button or two-button suit is de rigueur. If men choose to wear suits it is because they want to. If they decide to wear a pair of trainers with their suit that is also acceptable.

Menswear is not as trend focused as womenswear, but men and fashion designers alike have accepted that the male consumer is as scrupulous as any shopper. This means that the range of clothing available is huge, with no specific rules or regulations on shape, style or colour.

While the 1990s may have been overtly concerned with minimalism, the millennium signalled a demand for change. Since 2000 a shift in attitude has developed in dressing up or even dressing down. Now, men dress more individually than ever before, and they demand an eclectic mix of clothing options through which to communicate their personal vision.

Offering this variety is the current batch of contemporary designers who respect the traditions of menswear and its techniques and fuse it with a modern approach to design and innovation. Whether they embrace or rebel against tradition, the designers all share the appreciation of a contextual understanding of tailoring.

Since the 1970s there has been a growing emphasis on casual clothing as men have moved away from the conventions and associations of the suit. However, in contemporary menswear the casual debate is no longer a major issue. Some designers focus on smart garments while others celebrate casual clothing. The real discussion is concerned with communicating the essence of personal identity and style.

Sportswear is another important theme or reference in modern menswear with many designers using its associated fabrics, functions and details. Also, the juxtaposition of formal wear, sportswear and casual wear is a dominant theme as new solutions are created through hybrids of clothing genres.

Street style and the influence of music are deeply rooted in the psyche of contemporary menswear designers. Giving 'trivial' fashion a real identity or reason, music and street style allow fashion designers to avoid such whimsical associations as being overtly concerned with the male appearance.

POST-METROSEXUALITY, CONTEMPORARY MENSWEAR TACKLES ISSUES OF MASCULINITY, FEMININITY AND EVERYTHING IN BETWEEN. *As sexuality becomes less of an issue in society, menswear celebrates and supports this diversity. Men are definitely more aware of the way they look but are less concerned with gender.*

The PREOCCUPATION WITH YOUTH is a key theme in contemporary menswear. As a method of appearing modern, designers address youthful ways of dressing to CAPTURE THE ESSENCE OF NAIVETY. Looking as if you are not trying too hard is an important notion in menswear. While hanging luxurious clothing on skinny teenagers may seem obscure, the image of YOUTH AND YOUTHFULNESS HAS COME TO DEFINE MODERN MENSWEAR.

PAGE 8: SIV STØLDAL DESIGN STUDIO, 2007. *PAGE 9:* WALTER VAN BEIRENDONCK, SPRING/SUMMER 94. *LEFT:* SPASTOR, AUTUMN/ WINTER 06/07. *BELOW LEFT:* GASPARD YURKIEVICH STUDIO, 2007. *BELOW:* FRANK LEDER, AUTUMN/WINTER 03/04.

Another key element that defines contemporary menswear is the recurrent use of bold colour. Designers are no longer restrained by monochrome-focused collections, and many innovators have defined their design identity through the use of vibrant colour.

Milan and Paris are still regarded as the key capitals in menswear fashion design with both holding biannual fashion weeks. Milan promotes huge luxury brands that sell globally, while Paris also presents the powerful brands, but balances this with the promotion of creative fashion-forward designers. Paris is a podium for innovation.

New York offers important support to designers with a commercial sensibility as their driving force. The Council of Fashion Designers of America (CFDA) launched their fashion awards in 1986 to honour emerging talent. CFDA awards have been given to Marc Jacobs, Alexandre Plokhov for Cloak and Hedi Slimane for Dior Homme. Parsons School of Design in New York is accredited with providing new talents in fashion design, producing such alumni as Marc Jacobs and Rick Owens.

However it is Antwerp in Belgium and London that are paramount in informing the new contemporaries in menswear. Antwerp produced the Antwerp Six – Walter Van Beirendonck, Ann Demeulemeester, Dries Van Noten, Dirk Bikkembergs, Dirk Van Saene and Marina Yee – in the 1980s and their influence still resonates powerfully today. The Royal Academy of Fine Arts in Antwerp is central in coaching new creative designers such as Bernhard Willhelm and Raf Simons. Furthermore, Walter Van Beirendonck now teaches in the fashion department there and his influence is evident in the work of the graduates.

London, it seems, currently has the edge in creating new thinkers and radicals in menswear design. Although there is no established menswear fashion week in London, the UK capital is certainly producing the most exciting and innovative menswear designers.

Central Saint Martins College and the Royal College of Art (RCA) in London are playing an integral part in propelling menswear forward. The MA Menswear course at the RCA is the only course in the world to specialize in menswear design at Masters level. The two colleges aim to create a balance between individual expression and the global design context.

Ike Rust, senior menswear tutor at the RCA, sees London as very exciting at the moment. *'We have moved beyond the interesting lining and contrast prick-stitch brigade to really interesting menswear design. The best news is that menswear graduates are setting up their own design companies because they long to stay in London but have nowhere here that they want to work. This will have an enormous impact on the regeneration of menswear in London.'*

UK high-street store Topman has also helped to fuel the regeneration of menswear in London. *'We have been quietly supporting both established and fledgling menswear designers over the past five years or so through a number of initiatives,'* explains Topman's design director Gordon Richardson. Initially working with Kim Jones on a series of capsule collections when he was still establishing himself, Topman has since collaborated with Martin Andersson, Benjamin Kirchhoff and Ed Meadham and Peter Jensen on either specific product ranges or capsule collections. *'There has been a steady interest and focus on menswear, which I believe is healthier as it suggests longevity and future stability rather than being a flash-in-the-pan scenario,'* explains Richardson. *'There are so many good menswear designers operating, all they need is some sort of support to enable them to mature into future behemoths!'*

The MAN event in London, a collaboration between Topman and new-talent supporter Fashion East, was launched in 2005 and is now an established part of the London Fashion Week schedule. The event acts as a vehicle for expression and a platform for young menswear designers. MAN has successfully launched Benjamin Kirchhoff, Siv Støldal, Patrik Söderstam and Aitor Throup to a new generation of buyers.

The reason there is such a diversity of brands and ideas in contemporary menswear is that essentially men want to communicate something different about their individual style. Menswear is no longer status-led or solely rooted in tradition. It is driven by the personality of the consumer. Men will take elements from a range of designers and create a distinct personal style.

This book aims to show the diversity in clothing being produced by a selection of contemporary menswear designers. It is impossible to show every designer who is contributing to the field, but the book demonstrates the abundant range and innovation in modern menswear. It is futile to classify designers into those working in particular cities or types of design; instead the obvious route is to celebrate their identities, their differences and their individual creativity. Menswear now functions in parallel with womenswear. It is regarded as a creative and progressive industry that fuels the thirst for contemporary clothes. In the words of Ike Rust from London's Royal College of Art, *'What has actually happened is that womenswear is now so dull that it is creatively eclipsed by menswear.'*

ABOVE: IN 2007, THROUP PRESENTED AN INSTALLATION OF HIS GARMENTS AT MAN, AN EVENT DURING LONDON FASHION WEEK. *PAGES 12–13:* DURING HIS TIME AT THE ROYAL COLLEGE OF ART, THROUP WON MANY INDUSTRY AWARDS, INCLUDING THE EVISU 'FIGHTING COUNTERFEIT THROUGH DESIGN' COMPETITION. DRAWING IS AN ESSENTIAL PART OF HIS CREATIVE PROCESS.

AITOR THROUP

DRAWINGS THAT MUTATE INTO GARMENTS best describes the philosophy that fuels Aitor Throup's design process. With utilitarian clothing as a reference and ambitions to give each of his drawings an anatomy of their own, Throup elevates his clothing to contemporary visions. THROUP'S GARMENTS ARE PRECISELY CONSTRUCTED, FUNCTIONALLY SOUND AND THEY ALWAYS TELL A STORY.

Born in Argentina in 1980, Aitor Throup graduated from the Royal College of Art in London in 2006 with an MA in menswear design. While at college Throup won several fashion design awards from companies such as Umbro, Evisu and Levi's. At the international ITS#FIVE (International Talent Support) Fashion Awards for new talent in 2006, he won the prestigious Fashion Collection of the Year Award and also i-D magazine's Styling Award. Throup's graduate collection, entitled 'When Football Hooligans Become Hindu Gods', established his innovative approach to the design process and communication.

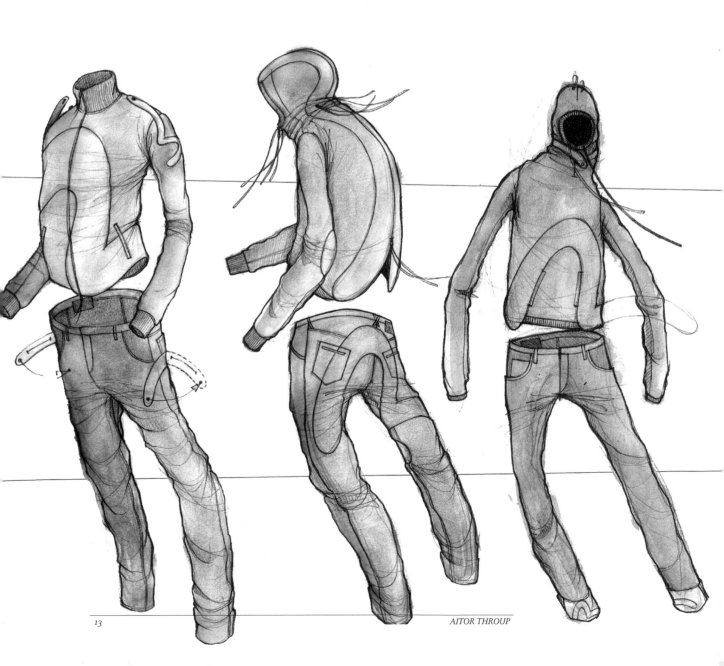

Anatomy and drawing are two of ***THROUP'S*** main passions. Through his clothing, he aims to create objects that possess their own physicality. He explores the human body in motion through drawings and this fascination is what eventually led him to work with clothing.

'My work is primarily about FINDING A REASON TO CREATE OR DESIGN ANYTHING. I am interested in justifying all design features and I avoid gratuitous detailing,' he explains.

Throup's design process is distinct and is what drives his work. *'For me, the most enjoyable part is probably being able to resolve the problem that the "concept" part of the process generates. My work could be described as a method of creating a truly original problem, and of resolving it in an equally original way. I believe this generates a truly innovative final product, as it wasn't conceived from an aesthetic, but rather from an idea, or a story.'* He first draws characters and then *'I convert those characters and their defining characteristics into wearable versions of themselves (the garment), so that any design features are dictated by the character and its relevance to the story. That's where the drawings come in. I don't believe in decorational values. I believe in origin, process and innovation.'*

During London Fashion Week in 2007, Throup launched his 'Aitor Throup Tailoring' concept, which revolves around a single outfit that is released every season based on a sculptural design process. Stemming from the same 'Justified Design' philosophy of his graduate collection, it is a showcase of an innovative three-stage design and cutting process. The first stage involves the drawing of a character. Then the character is sculpted in its original small scale and, finally, the sculpture is intricately covered in the garment's fabric, creating a unique construction pattern that is then enlarged in scale to fit the human body. *'The whole process becomes the product finally. When buying an "Aitor Throup Tailoring" suit, the package includes: a copy of the original drawing, a replica of the sculpture and, of course, the finished outfit.'*

This 'branding through construction' process allows Throup to realize his stories through clothes. He explains, *'All my shirts and jackets look like generic garments at first, but, on closer inspection, their construction lines are all equally distorted and seemingly misplaced.'*

Sports and military clothing is a clear inspiration for Throup and he cites Massimo Osti, founder of C.P. Company and Stone Island labels, as a major informer of his work. Elsa Schiapparelli, Martin Margiela, Carol Christian Poell, Hussein Chalayan and Leonardo da Vinci are also important inspirational figures.

OPPOSITE: A GARMENT IN THE PROCESS OF BEING CREATED FOR THROUP'S GRADUATION COLLECTION WHILST HE WAS STUDYING AT THE ROYAL COLLEGE OF ART (RCA) IN 2006. HE WAS AWARDED THE FASHION MENSWEAR AWARD BY THE RCA FOR HIS CONTEMPORARY PERSPECTIVE ON MENSWEAR DESIGN.

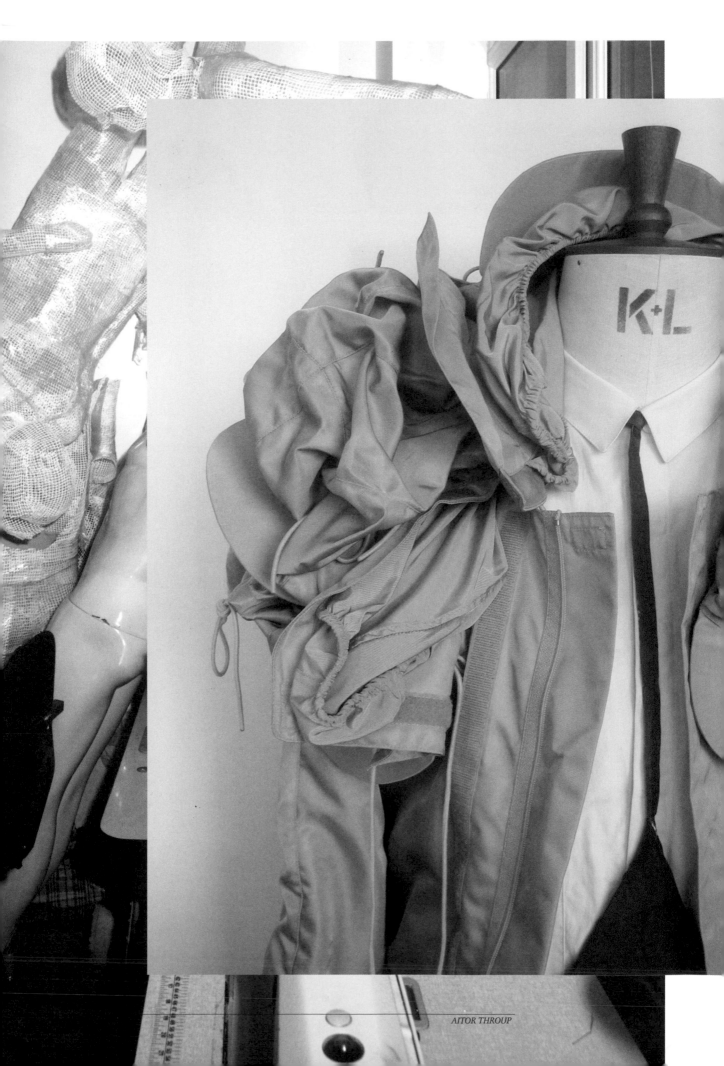

AITOR THROUP

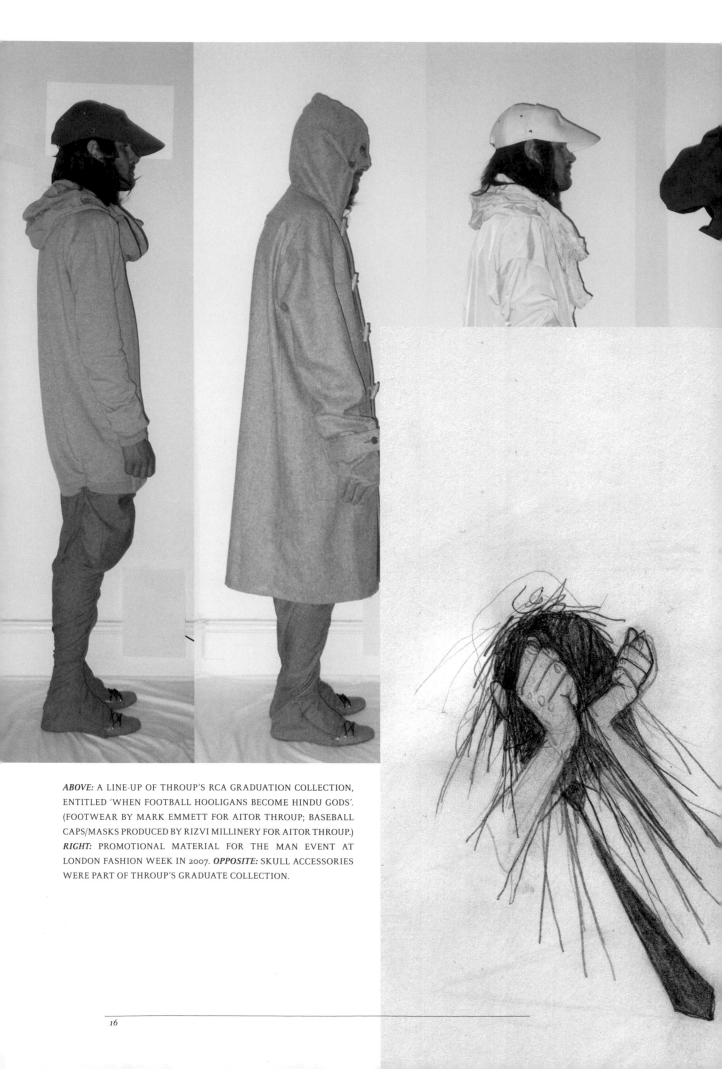

ABOVE: A LINE-UP OF THROUP'S RCA GRADUATION COLLECTION, ENTITLED 'WHEN FOOTBALL HOOLIGANS BECOME HINDU GODS'. (FOOTWEAR BY MARK EMMETT FOR AITOR THROUP; BASEBALL CAPS/MASKS PRODUCED BY RIZVI MILLINERY FOR AITOR THROUP.) *RIGHT:* PROMOTIONAL MATERIAL FOR THE MAN EVENT AT LONDON FASHION WEEK IN 2007. *OPPOSITE:* SKULL ACCESSORIES WERE PART OF THROUP'S GRADUATE COLLECTION.

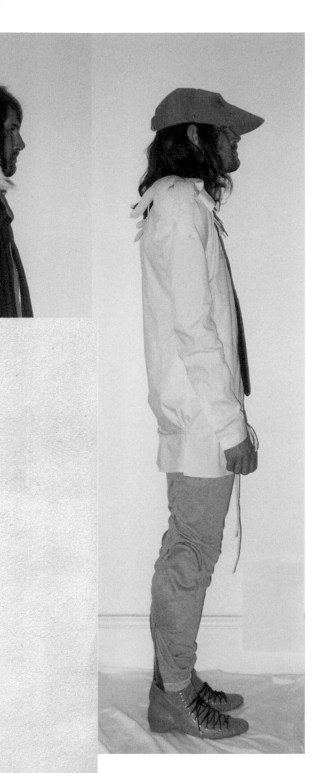

Throup believes his work appeals to a diverse audience. *'I like to think that it's difficult to pin-point my kind of customer, as there are no style or trend-led aesthetic or aspirational values attached to the core of my work. Overall, my customer will be somebody who may or may not be interested in fashion. My aim is to give as much, if not more, value to my products when viewed on a hanger as when seen on a human body.'*

Masculinity according to Throup is central to his work. *'For me, if a designer attempts menswear by disregarding or overlooking the relevance of their work to masculinity, then it won't be successful menswear. It's a menswear designer's responsibility to understand the context of his or her field, in order to explore or reinterpret it. It is impossible for a designer to redefine anything without understanding it first.'*

For Throup, successful menswear is not only capable of being wearable, functional, intricately detailed and relevant, but also of sustaining an uncompromised level of creative integrity. *'It seems to me that it is difficult for a lot of designers to communicate a truly original vision through menswear, as they feel they are impeded by the existing limitations of what is acceptable and successful in the menswear market. In my opinion, successful menswear has the confidence to detach itself from those misconceptions.'*

Although many of his contemporaries define their work by their aesthetic, Throup regards this as a futile exercise. *'I see too many new designers not achieving their full potential because all of a sudden their work is centred around this quest to achieve their own aesthetic. I think that design philosophies and processes should be defined, but aesthetics can change and evolve.'*

Throup's single-minded approach to menswear design champions the design process and simultaneously creates radical garments. His fearless perspective is intrepid and is recognized as a visionary method of working and thinking.

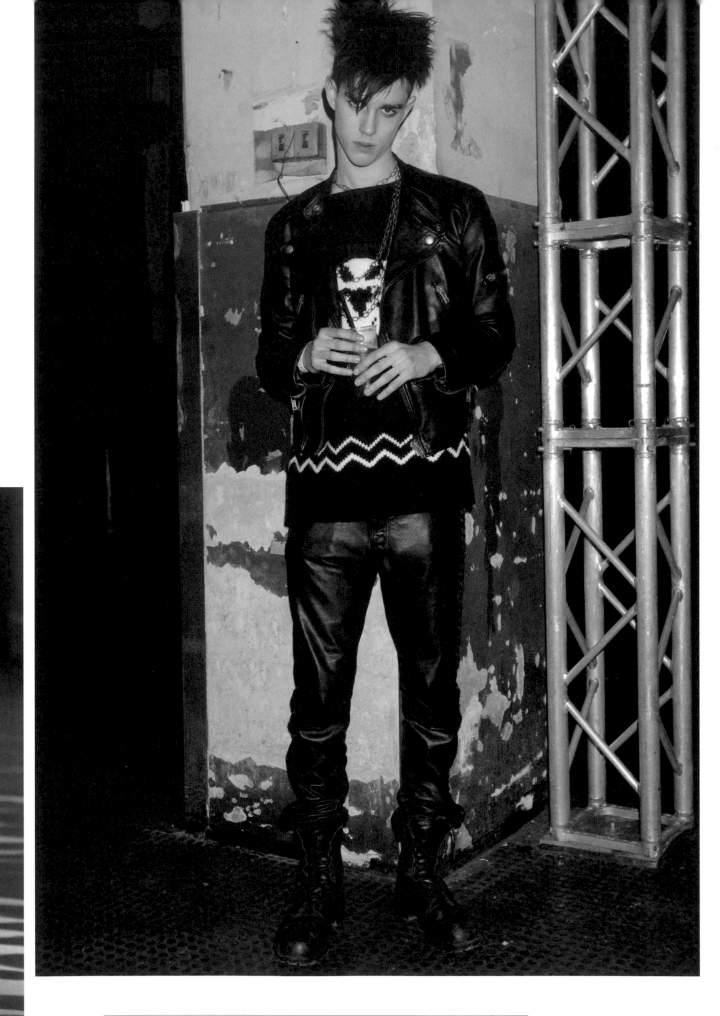

ALEXANDER McQUEEN

Since bursting onto the London fashion scene Alexander McQueen has embodied THE ESSENCE OF LONDON COOL. McQueen has a fearless attitude to fashion and its presentation; HIS INFLUENCE ON STYLE RESONATES GLOBALLY. As a notorious design creative and provocateur, his menswear never follows suit.

Regarded as one of the most innovative British designers working in fashion, Alexander McQueen creates challenging clothes and provocative presentations that have immense global influence and have made him a contemporary fashion icon. McQueen has developed a reputation for controversy and shock tactics and has been awarded the titles of 'enfant terrible' and 'the hooligan of English fashion'. Infamous for his 'bumster' trousers and aggressive tailoring skills, McQueen has always presented modern clothing in a defiant and progressive way.

THIS SPREAD: AUTUMN/WINTER 06/07 SAW THE LAUNCH OF MCQ – ALEXANDER McQUEEN, A DENIM-BASED READY-TO-WEAR LINE. THE LAUNCH TOOK PLACE IN AN OLD FACTORY IN MILAN THAT WAS FILLED WITH PINBALL AND GAMES MACHINES. TWELVE MODELS, PICKED FROM THE STREET, WERE FLOWN IN FROM LONDON AND POSTERS AROUND MILAN ADVERTISED THE LAUNCH.

ALEXANDER McQUEEN

Born in London in 1969, **_McQUEEN_** left school at the age of 16 and undertook an apprenticeship at the traditional Savile Row tailors Anderson & Shephard, followed by a period at neighbouring tailors Gieves & Hawkes. McQueen apparently graffitied his signature into the lining of the Prince of Wales's Savile Row jackets during his time in Savile Row. From there he moved to costumiers Angels & Bermans, where he mastered six methods of pattern cutting, from the melodramatic sixteenth-century shape to the sharp tailoring that has become his signature style.

At the age of 20 McQueen was employed by the fashion designer Koji Tatsuno, who shared McQueen's knowledge of and passion for British tailoring. A year later McQueen moved to Milan in Italy where he became design assistant to Romeo Gigli. In 1994 he returned to London to begin a Masters degree in fashion design at Central St Martins College. Isabella Blow, who championed the new designer as the saviour of British fashion, bought McQueen's degree collection in its entirety and catapulted his work into the international arena.

McQueen immediately launched his own label and went on to make a name for himself with such provocative collections as 'Nihilism' and 'Highland Rape'. His clothes are highly regarded for their sharp tailoring, technical excellence and intelligent interpretation of modern fashion. McQueen's early fashion shows became famous for communicating complex stories and powerful imagery, which often combined fantasy with disturbance and extreme beauty with aggression. He has always been focused on fusing the traditional skills of British tailoring with the fine workmanship of the French haute couture atelier and the flawless finish of Italian manufacturing.

In 1996, McQueen's fascination with couture was rewarded when he was appointed as chief designer at the French house of Givenchy, where he worked until March 2001. President Bernard Arnault of LVMH Moët Hennessy Louis Vuitton, of which Givenchy is a member company, caused controversy when he instated the relatively new and notorious British designer. McQueen refined his aggressive design aesthetic at Givenchy but still challenged the traditional perceptions of haute couture. In 1998, a show for his own label used car robots spraying paint over white cotton dresses and a disabled model marched down the catwalk on intricately carved wooden legs. In Givenchy couture shows, McQueen has used clear plastic mannequins to show the clothes instead of runway models. The mannequins were mounted in movable floors and their appearance on the stage was choreographed to music.

McQueen's design accomplishments have been recognized by the fashion industry. In 1996, 1997, 2001 and 2003, McQueen was awarded the prestigious British Designer of the Year. In 2003,

he was awarded the International Designer of the Year by the Council of Fashion Designers of America (CFDA) and, in the same year, he was presented with a CBE by Queen Elizabeth II. In 2004, he won British Menswear Designer of the Year.

In 2000, McQueen signed a new partnership with Gucci Group, through which he acquired 51% of the company and was employed as creative director. This has enabled him to expand into menswear and eyewear and become a global luxury label, launching fragrances and opening flagship stores in New York, London and Milan.

The Alexander McQueen menswear line was launched in 2004 and adhered to the same RADICAL CONCEPTS as have been associated with his womenswear. However, it also reflected McQueen's DESIGN MATURITY AND HIS ABILITY TO CREATE HIGHLY INVENTIVE YET WEARABLE CLOTHES.

As the backdrop for his first menswear show in Milan, McQueen chose an industrial building to create a minimal look. Models walked out from the darkness of the space into an austerely lit runway that stretched 120 metres (390 feet). This debut collection celebrated McQueen's tailoring and was inspired by 1930s army clothing, combined with Indian mirrored embroidery and henna tattooing. The models were paramount in communicating the vision: they were predominately cast from the street and included American soldiers and young London Asians.

Suzy Menkes, fashion editor of the *International Herald Tribune,* described the impact of McQueen's menswear debut. *'Alexander McQueen threw a grenade of actuality. Since McQueen is a showman, he included heads painted shocking pink and cobalt blue with Holi powder – or faces hidden in gas masks. But the clothes – a trench or Ghurka shorts in Madras check, military pants with a high-rise waistline and khaki-tailored shirts, including check piping around the edges – were sophisticated.'*

McQueen's design process is well documented. Films and historical stories frequently inspire him; his shows are often narrations of his inspiration and he feeds the audience his reference points. Shows are usually emotional and offer passionate views on his respect for the Arts and Crafts Movement.

Clearly a radical fashion innovator, McQueen has built a reputation through his menswear collections for pushing fashion forward and for offering contemporary visions for modern dressing.

ABOVE: EMBROIDERY AND HAND-CRAFTED DETAILS ARE CRUCIAL TO McQUEEN'S EXQUISITELY MADE CLOTHES, AS APPARENT IN THIS DETAIL FROM AUTUMN/WINTER 06/07. *LEFT:* McQUEEN WAS INSPIRED BY WILLIAM GOLDING'S *LORD OF THE FLIES* IN HIS SPRING/SUMMER 06 COLLECTION. AGAINST A BACKDROP OF DRAPED PARACHUTES, THE DESIGNER PRESENTED A COLLECTION OF EXPERTLY TAILORED CLOTHES.

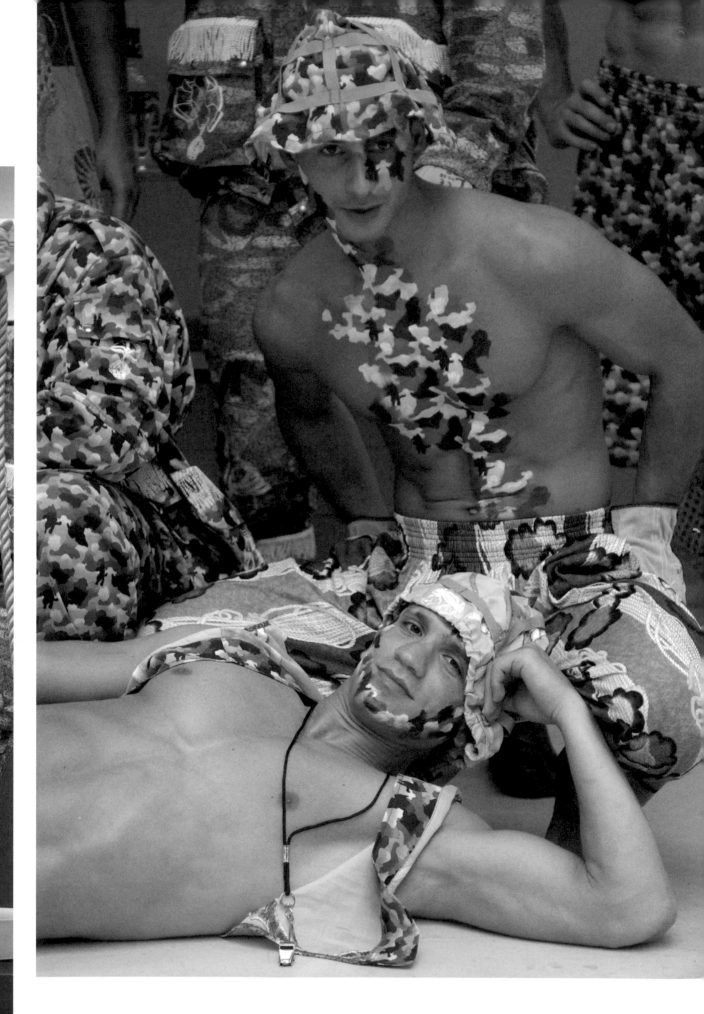

BERNHARD WILLHELM

Rebelling against the bland minimalism of the 1990s fashion scene, Bernhard Willhelm offers a new TECHNICOLOUR VISION. Patterned jumpsuits, white tracksuits, kaftans and gold bumbags have kick-started a new casual cool. SUBVERTING INFANTILE REFERENCES, Willhelm offers clothes that DEFY TRADITION and CAPTURE THE FASHION MOMENT.

Bernhard Willhelm was born in Germany in 1972. Whilst studying at the Royal Academy of Fine Arts in Antwerp, Belgium, Willhelm assisted Walter Van Beirendonck, Alexander McQueen, Vivienne Westwood and Dirk Bikkembergs. He graduated in 1998 and his collection entitled 'Le Petit Chapeau Rouge' earned him the Flanders Fashion Institute's prize of honour.

OPPOSITE: FOR HIS SPRING/SUMMER 04 COLLECTION, WILLHELM EXPLORED CAMOUFLAGE PATTERN AND ASSOCIATIONS WITH THE ARMY. IN THE SHOW, MODELS NAVIGATED THEIR WAY AROUND AN OBSTACLE COURSE, WHICH INCLUDED SWINGING OVER ARMY BUNK BEDS, UNDER TABLES AND THROUGH DOORS. *LEFT:* PATTERN, PRINT AND COLOUR ARE INTEGRAL TO WILLHELM'S PHILOSOPHY. IN HIS AUTUMN/WINTER 07/08 COLLECTION, HE CHALLENGED THE PERCEPTION OF TRADITIONAL MASCULINE GARMENTS BY CONTRASTING TAILORED TROUSERS WITH BAGGY OVERSIZED SPORTSWEAR JACKETS.

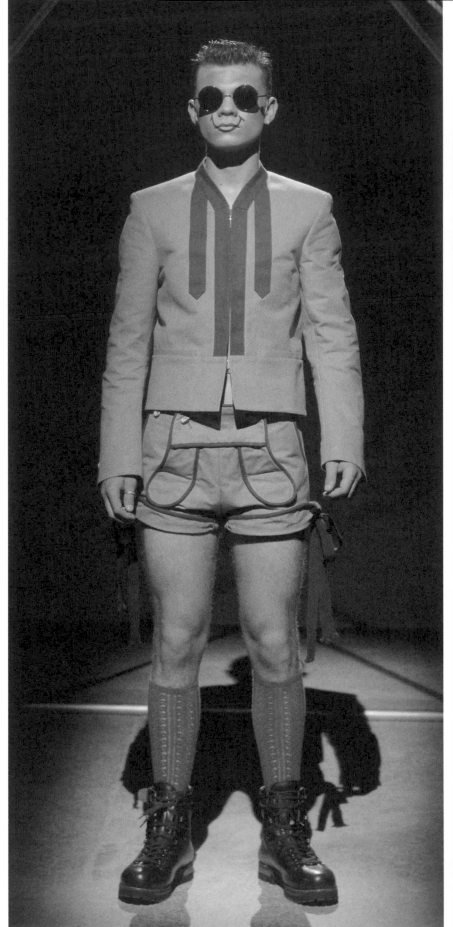

SUBVERTING TRADITIONAL MASCULINE CODES OF DRESS, WILLHELM DELIVERED A TECHNICOLOUR VISION FOR HIS SPRING/SUMMER 07 SHOW. NEON LIGHTING AND MODELS WITH PAINTED FACES ADDED TO THE DRAMATIC AND ENERGETIC PRESENTATION.

In 1999, _WILLHELM_ created his own label with business partner Jutta Kraus. He presented his first womenswear show in Paris in the same year, immediately attracting the attention of the fashion press for his edgy and challenging take on contemporary clothing, such as his bright experimental garments decorated with folklore motifs.

Willhelm's radical ideas can at times be difficult to comprehend. He is renowned for his progressive clothes, which are usually loud, bright and baggy. In rethinking traditional fashion shapes and ideas, Willhelm deconstructs the silhouette, then redesigns it according to his own rules. His garments question what is thought to be wearable and he pushes the boundaries of acceptable clothing.

Consistently innovative and humorous, Willhelm's fashion language is also sometimes cartoon-like. _'I'd say people know my work as being cool, naïve, German and exotic,'_ he explains, but goes on to admit that fashion was not his first career choice. _'I never wanted to do fashion. I never dressed my Barbie doll. I had a greenhouse at home, actually. I wanted to study medicine or something about plants. I really like nature.'_

Citing his native Bavaria as inspiration, Willhelm focuses on a new interpretation of folk-inspired clothes, traditional needlework and knitwear. His influences are as eclectic and dynamic as the garments he produces. He is informed by pop culture and his clothes always communicate a youthful playfulness. Other sources of inspiration include toys, computer games, Michael Jackson, McDonald's Happy Meal figures and dinosaurs. Willhelm believes that anything can be interesting – as long as you have a creative mind, you can do infinitely creative things.

Willhelm's design process is not formal. _'I don't make sketches; ideas come by doing things,'_ he explains. _'Concepts are boring; there's never a surprise with them.'_ Willhelm's work is experimental and has a lot to do with accidents. His studio will get an idea, then move on to the next, working on anything and everything simultaneously. He never thinks in terms of what specific garments are required but instead relishes the freedom of being able to do and design anything he wants. _'I don't like things that are literal. I'm spontaneous, greedy and I always want things.'_

In 2000, Willhelm launched his first menswear collection and presented his first menswear show in Paris in 2003. _'Menswear is about proportion, but I try to change that,'_ says Willhelm. His menswear collections are inspired by a pure abstract aesthetic. He describes it as an ideal image. The clothes are modern and do not suggest any relationship to traditional menswear. The shapes and fabrics of sportswear often inspire him and the collections usually reference sports garments, but the garments are transformed into contemporary and directional pieces. For his winter collection in 2005, Willhelm cast his black models in a Paris branch of Foot Locker. A heavy Nigerian influence was evident in the collection and the oversized silhouette of the clothes explored Willhelm's fascination with volume.

DIVERSITY and different groups of people also fascinate Willhelm. HE BELIEVES THAT EVERYONE IS EQUAL and that by aiming to understand different groups he can inform his design work and make it inspiring. He cites Arab and African communities as examples, describing how there is a huge sense of ENERGY THAT RESONATES FROM WITHIN THEIR SOCIAL GROUPS. Fashion according to Willhelm is part of culture and his work is concerned with challenging conformity.

From 2002 to 2004, Willhelm directed the Italian fashion house of Capucci, where he launched their first prêt-à-porter collection. A retrospective of his work was presented in 2003 at the Ursula Blickle Foundation for Contemporary Art in Germany. In 2005, Willhelm designed school uniforms for a school and orphanage run by Nestra Señora de Misericordia, an order of Benedictine nuns. In 2006, he launched his first shoe line, and created the 'White Wild Bunch', a clothing line only available through online store YOOX.com. The same year he also received the French ANDAM (National Association for the Development of Fashion Arts) Grand Prize for being the most promising talent of the new creative scene.

Willhelm has successfully captured the zeitgeist in contemporary menswear. He has the ability to create avant-garde designs, while presenting them as viable and wearable products. Many, especially the Japanese, love his whimsical, playful clothes that are infused with colour and dynamic shapes. Willhelm designs from within and he communicates very personal values on taste, dress codes and the conventions of society. In this way his clothes become three-dimensional tools that define our current society. On another level Willhelm, like many designers, finds simple pleasure in designing clothes that people connect with and enjoy wearing.

BLAAK

With 'non-colour' as inspiration for their clothes, the designers at Blaak translate their influences from a MEDLEY OF CULTURES AND TRADITIONS INTO DESIRABLE GARMENTS. Fusing traditional English tailoring techniques with the avant-garde, Blaak is at THE FOREFRONT OF CONTEMPORARY, YOUTHFUL CLOTHING.

London-based label Blaak was founded in 1998 by Aaron Sharif and Sachiko Okada. Both designers studied at Central St Martins College in London. The name of their label is a homage to the contemplation of emotions aroused by the colour black. 'The colour black has a transformative quality that symbolically purifies and regenerates, infinitely changing its meaning in time,' explains Okada, who along with Sharif has captured a committed following of customers who respond to their design philosophy.

FLORAL STRUCTURES AND SHAPES, BOTH RENDERED IN DELICATE PASTEL COLOURS, WERE TRANSLATED ON TO SHIRTS FOR BLAAK'S SPRING/SUMMER 07 COLLECTION.

The design duo made an immediate impact with their first collection, entitled 'Blaak Magic', which was inspired by the West, the East and Africa. They sold the collection to Browns in London, and then Liberty, Colette and Barneys, before they even graduated from college. Costume commissions soon followed from such celebrities as Madonna, Björk, Kylie Minogue, Moloko and David Bowie.

BLAAK'S debut at London Fashion Week came in 1999 with support from off-schedule initiative Fashion East. Their first scheduled show at London Fashion Week was in 2001 as part of the New Generation Designers Award sponsored by Marks & Spencer. In 2001 and 2002, they won the New Generation Award supported by the British Fashion Council, and in 2002 the *Elle* Style Young Designer of the Year Award. Vidal Sassoon awarded them the Cutting Edge Talent Award in 2002, and in 2004 they relocated their shows from London to Paris to reach a wider international audience.

OPPOSITE : FOR THEIR SPRING/SUMMER 07 COLLECTION, BLAAK WAS INSPIRED BY THE BASIC MAN'S SHIRT, WHICH BECAME A CANVAS THAT THEY EMBELLISHED WITH THEIR INNOVATION AND DESIGN CREATIVITY. *ABOVE:* FOR AUTUMN/WINTER 07/08, BLAAK DESIGNED DOUBLE-BREASTED SUITS THAT WERE INFORMED BY TRADITIONAL SHAPES. *PAGE 30:* ORNATE SHIRTS WERE A FOCUS FOR BLAAK'S AUTUMN/WINTER 07/08 COLLECTION. *PAGE 31:* TO GIVE THEIR SPRING/SUMMER 07 COLLECTION AN HISTORIC BUT CONTEMPORARY FEEL, BLAAK WORKED WITH BRITISH FACTORIES THAT USED TRADITIONAL MANUFACTURING TECHNIQUES.

The distinct design aesthetic of BLAAK DRAWS FROM DIVERSE WORLD CULTURES, reinterpreting tribal influences and using natural fabrics, such as leather and wool, in a FUSION OF HEDONISTIC STREET STYLE. They describe their look as 'SUBDUED ANARCHY'.

The most exciting aspect of design for Blaak is the thought process. Okada and Sharif relish the free-flowing ideas at the beginning of the process, before any commitment is made to fabric or silhouette. They describe the accumulation of ideas as 'THE DISTILLED CONCLUSION OF THE KALEIDOSCOPE OF THE MOMENT'. The team also cites several design icons, including 'the comedy of Azzedine Alaïa and the purity and sublime beauty of the Armani suit'.

Their early obsession with the colour black evolved quickly and the team increasingly began to use vibrant colour. Early collections featured both womenswear and menswear and referenced Blaak's expertise in cutting and tailoring techniques.

In menswear design, Blaak often explores the English gentleman's wardrobe. For example, a blazer reworked in leather, traditional mackintoshes and coats constructed with exaggerated round shoulders, and fitted jackets shown with extra-wide-leg trousers.

In 2007, Blaak launched their first stand-alone menswear collection entitled 'Boys Don't Cry'. It referenced the romance of the Edwardian period in England, and *'the soft melodic hues'* of David Hamilton's flower photography. The shirts were rendered in various fabrics, including denim, perforated and two-fold cottons and pinpoint oxford cloth, then embellished with Austrian lace, voile rose appliqués, tulle with Swarovski crystals, metal studs and polka dots covered with ivory voile. According to Okada, the collection was an ode to the iconic white button-down shirt, for its restraint against the freedom of conformity.

'Menswear has more restriction, and a more limited canvas on which to express itself. By limiting in one way, it allows us to go deeper in another way,' explains Okada on the decision to focus solely on menswear. The design team states that their menswear philosophy is inspired by *'The Working Class Hero, The Poet, The Outsider, Edwardian Pomp and Ceremony with a whispered subversive punch. The obsession with The Cut.'*

Contemporary men's clothing, according to Blaak, should be *'Open to suggestion; the mould, the rule book, the ideal is broken and all the fragments have their chance to coexist. There is no code of dress. Confidence in one's own conviction and determination makes contemporary now.'*

Masculinity is also a key factor for the design team. *'It's ingrained within our minds, our society. It's such a potent force, that its importance is customary. Having said that, we try to work with this idea by working against it.'*

Blaak's respect for tradition and for classic menswear garments resonates throughout their work. By reworking and pushing conventions, shapes and garments, the team presents modern ideas. Making the most impossible, the most subtle ideas work is a challenge. *'Menswear is a gradual process, a world where ideas are reflected over and condensed into final forms that can coexist with what preceded and entice.'*

Sharif and Okada believe menswear is successful when a conversation is created between the design team and its audience. For them, a garment is only really complete when it is being worn by someone. *'Our customer is a person that understands the riot of anarchy, the need for the whimsical and the hidden fine lines bound in society.'*

BURBERRY PRORSUM

Burberry is one of the largest fashion brands in the world. British designer Christopher Bailey has transformed the company into an INTERNATIONAL AND INFLUENTIAL POWERHOUSE.

The Burberry brand has an impressive history. Established in 1856 by Thomas Burberry, the company opened its first Burberry shop in Hampshire, England, selling country clothes to the landed gentry. In 1891, the first London store opened and by 1895 Burberry was creating uniforms for the British military.

OPPOSITE: THE SPRING/SUMMER 98 ADVERTISING CAMPAIGN ILLUSTRATES BURBERRY'S HERITAGE, WHICH IS ROOTED IN OUTDOOR CLOTHING, SPECIFICALLY THE MAC. *BELOW:* IMAGES FROM THE BURBERRY ARCHIVE. *RIGHT:* LORD LICHFIELD CREATED SOME OF THE DEFINING IMAGES FOR THE BRAND, BOTH AS A PHOTOGRAPHER AND IN FRONT OF THE CAMERA AS A MODEL IN ADVERTISEMENTS.

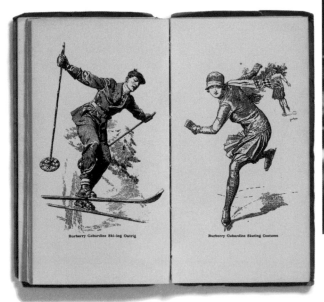

BURBERRY check or plaid was originally used as the lining for trench coats in 1924, and the garment was turned into a classic by Humphrey Bogart in the film *Casablanca*. Burberry's reputation for innovation was established when they patented gabardine, a water-resistant material that came to characterize their famous mac. In 1955, Burberry received a Royal Warrant from Queen Elizabeth II.

In 1999, the high-end fashion-focused Burberry Prorsum women's line was launched and a year later the men's line followed. Christopher Bailey was appointed as design director in 2001 and the Burberry fashion revolution began. Responsible for the contemporary direction of the Prorsum label, Bailey has propelled the brand into the consciousness of the fashion hierarchy. Prorsum, the company's motto, is Latin for 'forward', and since Bailey's arrival Burberry has celebrated a rejuvenation in contemporary clothing.

Born in 1971, Bailey graduated from the BA Fashion Design course at the University of Westminster in 1990, before attending the Royal College of Art, graduating in 1994. Moving to New York, Bailey worked for Donna Karan before becoming senior designer for Gucci womenswear in 1996.

When *Forbes* magazine published a list of the world's most influential designers in November 2005, Christopher Bailey was at the top, generating £170 million in sales at Burberry and getting 421 press mentions during the year. Bailey was also awarded Designer of the Year at the British Fashion Awards in the same year.

Bailey is responsible for making Burberry Prorsum desirable, modern and luxurious. The label is the perfect example of the 'Englishness' celebrated at the 'AngloMania' exhibition at The Metropolitan Museum of Art in New York in 2006, sponsored by Burberry to celebrate their 150th anniversary.

TOP: COLOUR IS A KEY ELEMENT TO THE SUCCESS OF THE BURBERRY PRORSUM BRAND. THE SPRING/SUMMER 05 COLLECTION FLOODED THE CATWALK WITH SHADES FROM BLAZING ORANGE TO PILLAR-BOX RED. *LEFT*: IN HIS AUTUMN/WINTER 05/06 COLLECTION, CHRISTOPHER BAILEY NODDED TO THE LATE 1960S, WHEN LONDON'S KING'S ROAD WAS THE CENTRE OF GLOBAL STYLE. THE SIGNATURE BURBERRY TRENCH COAT WAS DESIGNED IN LAMINATED COTTON TO MODERNIZE THE PATTERN. *OPPOSITE, BACK:* FOR AUTUMN/WINTER 07/08, BURBERRY PRORSUM FOCUSED ON A SHARP NARROW-LEG SILHOUETTE. *OPPOSITE, FRONT:* DISHEVELLED ELEGANCE WAS BAILEY'S THEME FOR THE BURBERRY PRORSUM SPRING/SUMMER 07 COLLECTION. SHIRTS WITH PLEATED FRONTS, TROUSERS WITH BEADED STRIPES AND COATS WITH OVERSIZED BUTTONS WERE PRESENTED IN A PREDOMINANTLY WHITE COLOUR PALETTE.

In directing this essentially English brand, Bailey has successfully fused his YOUTHFUL INNOVATIVE DESIGN sensibilities with commerce. The Prorsum line has added a LUXE EDGE to Burberry's functional portfolio. CLEAN LINES, CLASSIC STYLE AND A SOPHISTICATED PALETTE OF CONTEMPORARY COLOURS define the Prorsum collection, which is regarded as modern but ALWAYS WEARABLE. Burberry Prorsum is also concerned with being SLIGHTLY DIVERSE and is seen as HIGHLY FRESH AND DIRECTIONAL WITHOUT EVER BEING TOO AVANT-GARDE.

English icons are often cited by Bailey as inspiration for his menswear. Figures such as Princes William and Harry at the Royal Military Academy Sandhurst, interior designer David Hicks and photographers Lord Snowdon and Patrick Lichfield have all informed Bailey's collections. The Prorsum line is often seen as a wardrobe for an eccentric aristocrat or creative English gentleman.

Embracing the heritage of the house of Burberry has allowed Bailey to transform the brand into a highly successful business. Trench coats have always been integral to both the Burberry brand and to the directional attitude of Prorsum. Bailey reinvents this staple garment each season, updating it so it always appears contemporary and new. Details such as big buttons or oversized shoulder flaps modernize this traditional piece.

The debut Prorsum menswear collection by Bailey was presented in Milan in 2002. The clothes were gothic inspired and signalled a move away from the house check. References to Burberry heritage were subtle and suggested a new direction for the label.

In 2003, the Prorsum collection was pushed further in terms of contemporary fashion design. Colour and pattern, for which Bailey has become renowned, were explored in a confident presentation. The house check was enlarged and used on skinny knits and pants in cotton and lurex.

Bailey's confident use of colour has defined the Prorsum brand. He has developed a sophisticated language that always communicates a fresh and modern approach to menswear. With a sensibility that never appears too directional or too avant-garde, Bailey has ensured that the Prorsum brand is always obtainable: it has a sense of charm and wearability that appeals to a wide consumer audience.

OPPOSITE: SUBVERTING AND UPDATING THE BURBERRY CHECK HAS BEEN INTEGRAL TO BAILEY'S APPROACH TO THE BRAND. THIS PIECE IS FROM THE BURBERRY PRORSUM AUTUMN/WINTER 03/04 COLLECTION. *LEFT:* THE BURBERRY PRORSUM AUTUMN/ WINTER 07/08 COLLECTION WAS DESCRIBED BY THE DESIGNER AS FORMAL BUT STILL BASED ON THE IDEA OF A SCRUFFY ENGLISH KID.

COSMIC WONDER
LIGHT SOURCE

IN 2007, COSMIC WONDER'S ELUSIVE CREATOR Yukinori Maeda announced a change in strategy. Cosmic Wonder was divided into three projects, which would be guided in distinctly different ways to build a more tangible framework within which Yukinori believed he could communicate his concepts. The trio are Cosmic Wonder, COSMIC WONDER Light Source and the artworks he produces under his own name.

'Commitment to the concept' describes the evolving collections created under the Cosmic Wonder umbrella. COSMIC WONDER Light Source is the new and only clothing project, developed by Yukinori 'To clothe everyday life. We introduced COSMIC WONDER Light Source to encourage people to wear these clothes in their daily life, so that we may delight in discovering anew the spirit within us.'

OPPOSITE: A SLEEPING-BAG INSTALLATION ENTITLED 'HIDDEN PATH OF LIGHT' BY COSMIC WONDER 2006 COMMUNICATES YUKINORI'S FOCUS ON ART. *LEFT:* 'HOUSE' BY YUKINORI MAEDA 2003, A PLYWOOD AND FLUORESCENT LIGHT ARTWORK. *ABOVE:* AN OUTFIT FROM COSMIC WONDER JEANS' AUTUMN/WINTER 05/06 COLLECTION, SHOWING A MORE WEARABLE APPROACH TO DESIGN WHILE STILL RETAINING THE BRAND'S AESTHETIC.

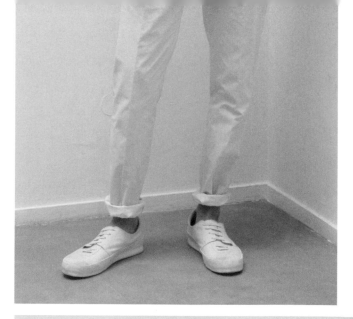

Now based in Japan, Yukinori studied architecture before he started **_COSMIC WONDER_** and later the more wearable Cosmic Wonder Jeans. In recent years, he has been actively creating and exhibiting his personal artworks in parallel with his works for Cosmic Wonder. Yukinori exhibited at the MU Art Foundation in Eindhoven, The Netherlands in 2005, San Francisco's Yerba Buena Center for the Arts in 2006 and the Museum of Contemporary Art in Tokyo in 2007.

Cosmic Wonder debuted in Paris in 2000 at the Centre Pompidou during Paris Fashion Week, and this has remained the principal forum for presenting Cosmic Wonder's work. Cosmic Wonder has developed to take on a wider focus to further its exploration of installation and performance in venues around the world. Works in various media such as sculpture, clothing, film, photography and music have been developed exclusively in limited-edition formats. The emphasis and philosophy of the activities are rooted deeply in artistic expression.

Yukinori's clothes are informed by eclectic references. Previous inspirations include white magic, mysticism, collegiate codes and folklore. Originality and wit are always key to the collections as Yukinori has created a distinct brand, which encompasses challenging philosophies that are translated into inherently modern garments.

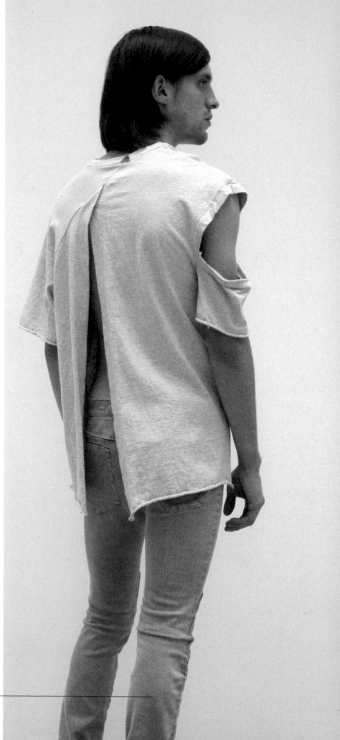

OPPOSITE, LEFT: AN INSTALLATION IN THE COSMIC WONDER SHOP, TOKYO, 2007. OPPOSITE, RIGHT COLUMN: MINIMAL GARMENTS IN PALE COLOURS FROM COSMIC WONDER LIGHT SOURCE'S SPRING/ SUMMER 07 COLLECTION. ABOVE: AN OUTFIT INCORPORATING DRIFTWOOD FROM COSMIC WONDER'S PERFORMANCE ENTITLED 'ECLIPSE', 2006.

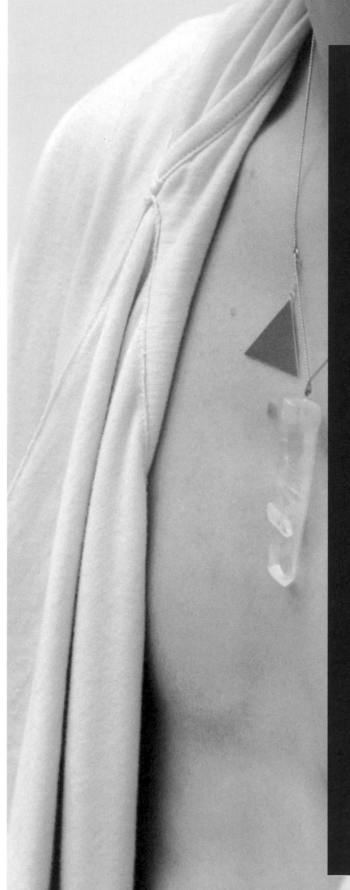

1. *HOW WOULD YOU DESCRIBE YOUR CREATIVITY?*
    'I have three projects. They are Cosmic Wonder, COSMIC
    WONDER Light Source and Yukinori Maeda. Cosmic Wonder,
    which I would call neither art nor fashion, is a means to pass
    along a new sense of values and propose another way of seeing
    the world by linking together diverse modes of expression. As
    Yukinori Maeda, I make artworks. COSMIC WONDER Light
    Source is my sole fashion project. Distinct processes guide these
    three projects, and so they vary the flow of my daily work.'

2. *DESCRIBE YOUR MENSWEAR DESIGN PHILOSOPHY.*
    'It begins with a concept: create a space and bring the space
    with you every day. COSMIC WONDER Light Source is a new
    fashion project of Cosmic Wonder. I believe that the collec-
    tions of COSMIC WONDER Light Source will allow people to
    delight in discovering anew the spirit within us. Wearing the
    clothes is a way of bringing this joy into one's daily life.
    COSMIC WONDER Light Source is a collection for transform-
    ing one's everyday movements into spatial expression.'

3. *WHAT IS THE MOST ENJOYABLE PART OF DESIGN?*
    'The moment when energy is released and I feel it is infinite.'

4. *DOES YOUR DESIGN PROCESS ALWAYS FOLLOW THE
    SAME ROUTE?*
    'Each follows its own route.'

5. *WHO ARE YOUR DESIGN ICONS?*
    'Light. The concept is to wear light and, in so doing, to create
    an environmental effect. When I say light, there are many
    different kinds of light: the human body, spirit and soul can
    also be seen as light. This kind of light is very precious and
    very important to us right now.'

OPPOSITE: THE COSMIC WONDER LIGHT SOURCE SPRING/SUMMER
COLLECTION 07 FOCUSED ON LIGHT FABRICS IN SOFT COLOURS.

ABOVE: A DOUBLE SLEEVE SHIRT ADDS HUMOUR TO THE COSMIC
WONDER JEANS' AUTUMN/WINTER 05/06 COLLECTION.

COSTUME NATIONAL

Combining tailoring, technology and couture, Costume National creates an URBAN AND MODERN WARDROBE FOR MEN. Using military uniforms as a starting point, the label builds on an EASTERN DESIGN AESTHETIC by adding a EUROPEAN MODERNITY. SHARPLY SLICED SILHOUETTES are often extreme but always controlled, creating garments with a DYNAMIC FASHION LANGUAGE.

The designer and founder of Costume National, Ennio Capasa, was born in Lecce in Puglia, Italy, in 1960. His parents ran a fashion boutique called Smart in the 1950s, and when he was 18 he spent a year travelling extensively through the Far East. Capasa went on to study sculpture at Milan's Academia di Brera, returning to Japan in 1982 to work for Yohji Yamamoto after a friend sent the designer some of Capasa's illustrations. This was where Capasa learned how to pare down design details and use traditional cutting techniques as a driving force for his silhouettes.

A YOUTHFUL PERSPECTIVE DEFINES THE COSTUME NATIONAL LOOK FOR SPRING/SUMMER 07. CONTEMPORARY FABRICS ARE A KEY PART OF THE DESIGNER'S VISION. CAPASA IS RENOWNED FOR HIS DISTINCT MINIMALIST STYLE, IN THIS CASE PURE WHITE.

In 1986, Capasa returned to Milan to start his own label, Costume National, a name inspired by a book of uniforms. He launched the collection in collaboration with his brother, Carlo, who had worked with Romeo Gigli and Gucci. The first ready-to-wear and shoe collection for women was launched in 1987. It fused Japanese purism with a sexier, contemporary silhouette informed by Western dress codes and an appreciation of innovative street style.

Soon realizing that Milan was not the optimum place to receive recognition for this modern edgy aesthetic, Capasa and his team moved to Paris in 1991. His mentor, Yamamoto, was already showing there and Capasa felt his own directional vision would be appreciated in the cosmopolitan French capital. It was in Paris that the fashion press and buyers supported the womenswear collections, and so in 1993 Capasa decided to launch a menswear range. *'In the early 1990s, when I reinvented the male silhouette, my inspiration came from the great romantics, like Byron, Shelley, Baudelaire and Rimbaud for their lean and modern elegance,'* explains Capasa. *'And today this remains unchanged. Their legacy is what has eventually become the soul of Costume National Homme.'*

In 2002, Costume National launched a range of fragrance and beauty products, followed by eyewear in 2003. The company runs its own shoe factory in northern Italy, and also has a leather-treatment factory for dyeing leather. Costume National's footwear business now represents one-third of all its international sales. There are Costume National Collection stores in Tokyo, Rome, New York and other major cities around the world.

Capasa also designs costumes for stage and film, comes up with the concept for CNC's stores and creates art exhibitions. In 2002, he designed a show at Milan's Pavilion of Contemporary Art, which featured works from revered artists Louise Bourgeois and Cindy Sherman.

As a dedicated fashion modernist, Capasa has successfully combined the purity of Japanese design with an edgy European aesthetic. The result is clothes for men that are practical, contemporary and directional.

Capasa found it difficult to find clothes that he liked for himself, so he created a very personal vision. The label became known for promoting the 'NEW ITALIAN DESIGN' movement, which is concerned with presenting HYPERMODERN AND INNOVATIVE CLOTHING. Capasa's collections have successfully reinvented classic shapes and presented them as modern pieces that resonate with an urban toughness.

Capasa's work has since been characterized by his architectural precision in draping fabric. His design aesthetic blends precise cutting techniques with impeccable tailoring skills and an ability to design garments that are both modern but wearable and youthful. His men's collections are inherently progressive and while they hint at traditional menswear shapes they always capture the current mood in fashion.

When presenting his vision, Capasa often uses contemporary synthetic fabrics and, because of this, his clothes are renowned for their practicality and distinct minimalist style. *'I have an increasing desire for things that are simple and sexy,'* he states. *'I like larger volumes, very light fabrics and a true sense of freedom. Jackets and trousers that are so perfectly cut as to be formal and yet very easy. So light that sometimes they make you think you are naked.'*

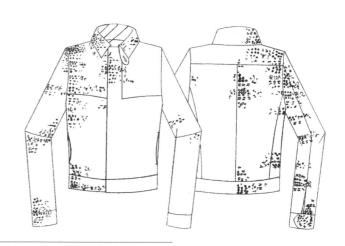

OPPOSITE: A SKETCH FOR A JACKET. *THIS PAGE:* CAPASA'S WORK IS DEFINED BY HIS ARCHITECTURAL PRECISION IN CUTTING AND DRAPING FABRIC. COLLECTIONS ARE MODERN IN THEIR APPROACH AND ALWAYS CAPTURE THE CURRENT MOOD IN FASHION, AS SHOWN IN THESE GARMENTS FROM THE SPRING/ SUMMER 07 RANGE.

D SQUARED2

SATIRICAL STORIES fuel the high-energy fashion shows of D Squared2. With a design philosophy that blatantly celebrates the male physique, the Caten twins design clothes that DEFINE WEARABILITY. The label has captured a distinct energy in contemporary menswear, with Italian tailoring at its core and masses of CHEEKY INNUENDOS.

Canadian identical twin brothers Dean and Dan Caten form D Squared2. Leaving their home country in 1991, they moved to Milan with ambitions to design their own fashion collection. The result was a debut in 1994 with a men's collection that spurred a movement in menswear design to celebrate masculinity and wearable clothes. Since their arrival in the Italian fashion capital, they have successfully portrayed a hedonistic attitude to men's fashion and its promotion.

OPPOSITE: DEAN AND DAN CATEN THRIVE ON FLAUNTING THE MALE PHYSIQUE IN THEIR COLLECTIONS. FOR THEIR SPRING/ SUMMER 07 SHOW THEY FOCUSED ON SPORTSWEAR, WITH THE CLOTHES REFERENCING YACHTING, SWIMMING, BOXING AND TRACK AND FIELD EVENTS. THE COLLECTION MADE THE CROSSOVER FROM SPORTSWEAR TO HIGH FASHION. **THIS PAGE:** IMAGES FROM LOCKER ROOMS INSPIRED THE SPRING/SUMMER 07 COLLECTION.

Super-low-slung jeans and body-conscious clothing define the **D SQUARED2** aesthetic, classified by a unique mix of North American wit, refined Italian tailoring and an attention to design detail. *'We consider our clothes to be real,'* explains Dean Caten, *'Simple, straightforward and down to earth. We want people to look cool, not dressed up and we design what we want to wear ourselves.'* Integral to the success of the label is their take on irony and humour. Their high-octane, testosterone-fuelled shows and their non-conformist attitude to men's fashion have set them apart from other concept-driven designers.

The D Squared2 fashion shows are often multimedia extravaganzas, combining fashion with art and music. Dean and Dan have collaborated with the photographer Steven Klein to develop a series of images for advertising campaigns that express their pure ideals of sensuality and masculinity.

The label's modern wearability has attracted a celebrity following that includes Lenny Kravitz, Justin Timberlake and Ricky Martin. The twins were commissioned to create costumes for Madonna's 'Don't Tell Me' video and the cowboy segment in her 2002 'Drowned World' tour. *'The Madonna thing was a big deal for us, because she has always been a huge inspiration. She first liked a pair of our jeans and before we knew it we had created 150 pieces for her tour. It has been an amazing and fulfilling experience,'* says Dean Caten. Hip-hop singer Eve also generated press for the brothers when she wore D Squared2 to accept the Breakthrough Style Award at the 2002 VH-1/*Vogue* Fashion Award Show.

Consequently, the brothers previewed their Spring/Summer 03 menswear collection with an unexpected twist by unveiling nine looks from their debut women's collection. The following day, the influential US fashion newspaper *Women's Wear Daily* featured the designers on its cover and published a two-page interview. Dean explains, *'The women's collection completely embraces the D Squared2 spirit. It is vibrant, confident, fun and effortlessly cool. We feel it is a perfect complement to our signature men's look.'*

It is, however, with the men's collection that D Squared2 have made their name, and it is their distinct approach to design that makes their clothes so popular. *'Some fashion gets too much like costume,'* says Dan. *'We are not about that. The attitude is the same in each collection. It's about not taking it all too seriously.'*

The twins' design philosophy is clear. They are concerned with PROPORTION, CUT, FIT and FORMS THAT ALWAYS FOLLOW FUNCTION. A DESIGN EDGE is paramount with both QUALITY and FUNCTIONALITY. By rearranging some of the rules and by playing with proportion and colour, D Squared2 offers something that can be rare in contemporary menswear, namely CASUAL AND VERY WEARABLE clothes that have a UNIQUE SENSE OF HUMOUR.

Dean and Dan are driven by a specific theme each season and this narrative is followed through to the presentation of the show. *'A theme fuels the process; it's the point of departure and everything else runs off it,'* explains Dean. *'It is important in being creative but without being excessive. We aim always to get the balance right.'* Inspirations for collections are varied and always portrayed with a humorous slant; recent catalysts have included cowboys, trailer parks, truck stops, motocross and Alpine skiing holidays. The designers are respected for their lean tailored jackets and outerwear, tight T-shirts and low-cut trousers, worn by customers who are sexually aware and confident. Always sexy and frequently theatrical, D Squared2 garments are also sometimes extreme but are easy to incorporate into a modern wardrobe.

Successful menswear, according to D Squared2, is fine tuned, focused, full of interesting details and well fitting. Defining masculinity is also key to their look. *'It is menswear so we believe the key word is most definitely "menswear". The D Squared2 man is very much a man's man and that's how we represent him in our collections. Our customer is loyal and faithful, confident and strong. Our customer expects the best and that's what we give him.'*

The Caten twins enjoy realizing the final products and design clothes with a view to making them very wearable and very desirable. They see contemporary menswear as diverse and that is its strength. *'There is no one specific direction,'* says Dean. *'Everybody is individual and everyone should learn to embrace their own individuality.'*

A FUR-TRIMMED COAT FROM THE AUTUMN/WINTER 07/08 COLLECTION SHOWS HOW D SQUARED2 FUSES FUNCTIONAL SPORTSWEAR WITH LUXURIOUS MATERIALS.

DIOR HOMME

A RAZOR-SHARP AESTHETIC defines the Dior Homme line. Revolutionizing menswear design, the label is regarded as the MOST INFLUENTIAL of its generation. With a monochrome palette and an explicit and slick look, Dior Homme has come to PERSONIFY MODERN MENSWEAR.

The popularization of the skinny silhouette in contemporary menswear can be accredited to Hedi Slimane, the influential designer behind Dior Homme between 2000 and 2007. By fusing a style union between music and fashion, Dior Homme has become the ultimate fashion brand that defines the youth generation.

OPPOSITE: FOR HIS SPRING/SUMMER 07 COLLECTION AT DIOR HOMME, HEDI SLIMANE WAS INSPIRED BY YOUTH CULTURE AND SUBCULTURES. THE CLOTHES WERE A CONTEMPORARY AND EDGY MIX OF BLACK HIGHLIGHTED WITH SILVER METALLICS. **LEFT:** ON THE CATWALK, ULTRA-SKINNY MODELS WERE STYLED WITH FLOPPY FRINGES TO CONTINUE SLIMANE'S EXPLORATION OF YOUTHFULNESS IN THE SPRING/SUMMER 07 COLLECTION.

ABOVE: SLIMANE WAS KNOWN FOR HIS SHARP TAILORING AND SLIM SILHOUETTES AT DIOR HOMME. THIS OUTFIT IS FROM THE AUTUMN/WINTER 03/04 COLLECTION. OPPOSITE: DIOR HOMME CHAMPIONS THE HYPER-ATTENUATED SILHOUETTE, THE MONO-CHROME PALETTE AND THE IMPECCABLE COUTURE FINISH. THE SUIT IS FROM THE SPRING/SUMMER 07 COLLECTION.

Slimane was born in 1968 in Paris. He studied art history at the Ecole du Louvre in Paris, and then trained as a tailor. From 1992 to 1995, Slimane worked as assistant to Jean-Jacques Picard on several fashion projects, including the centenary of the monogram by Louis Vuitton. From 1997, he designed for Yves Saint Laurent Rive Gauche Homme and, in 2000, Slimane became creative director at **_DIOR HOMME_**.

Under Slimane's direction, the label was transformed into a cutting-edge brand that honours modernity. The debut collection was announced as *'a new way to be masculine',* and Slimane went on to create one of the most identifiable and influential vocabularies in contemporary menswear.

MONOCHROME PALETTES, HYPER-SKINNY SILHOUETTES and SHARP CUTTING have created a distinct look that has been appropriated by the mass market. Slimane said at the time of the launch that his collection was about a VERY HEDONISTIC MOMENT IN TIME and about an IMMEDIATE PLEASURE. Slimane successfully captured the zeitgeist of the time; his clothes were an INSTANT SUCCESS and PROPELLED the brand to GLOBAL RECOGNITION.

In September 2001, Slimane was awarded the Man of the Year Award for emerging talent by American *GQ* magazine, and in April 2002 he was named International Designer of the Year by the Council of Fashion Designers of America (CFDA).

Slimane does not regard his job as just designing clothes. His creative projects include art, interior design, graphics and photography. He designed ebony and stainless-steel furniture that was sold at Dover Street Market in London, and he undertook a residency at Berlin's Kunst-Werke Institute for Contemporary Art. Berlin was the subject of his first book, and the slim look of the young students in the German capital inspired many of his collections.

It was this use of very young and thin models that made Dior Homme's shows notorious. He cast his models from the streets of London and Berlin to adhere to the look of his collection. His obsession with their ultra-skinny physiques caused controversy in the fashion industry. Many journalists reported that his clothes were unsuitable for the average man and feminized masculinity. The debate only created more focus on the brand and further promoted the Dior Homme look.

For Slimane, inspiration is intrinsically linked to the world of music. He has worked closely with the Libertines, Franz Ferdinand, Bloc Party and Razorlight. Slimane has supported the regeneration of British rock and it is this rock'n'roll aesthetic that has continually informed his designs. His most controversial muse is Pete Doherty of Baby Shambles, who Slimane describes as having effortless cool. Slimane was inspired by the intimacy and directness of

Doherty's live performance and produced a book in homage to his muse entitled *London: Birth of a Cult*. A photograph taken by Slimane captures Doherty in a slashed white T-shirt cut to the chest, and the same look is evident in Dior Homme's Spring/Summer 06 collection.

Unlike many designers who are fanatical about dressing celebrities, Slimane insists that he does not want to dress them, but instead he wants them to tell him what he can do for them. He believes they know exactly what they want, but that for his role to succeed he needs to understand their performance and body language. For Slimane it is a more collaborative process, a two-way act in which both parties participate.

In turn, Dior Homme is now patronized by many in the music industry: Mick Jagger, David Bowie, Elton John, Bryan Ferry, Jake Shears of the Scissor Sisters, Thurston Moore of Sonic Youth and Alex Kapranos of Franz Ferdinand are all Dior Homme addicts. Slimane has also attracted Hollywood luminaries, with Brad Pitt, Orlando Bloom and Ewan McGregor all adopting Dior Homme's signature skinny silhouettes.

By styling the rock industry and everybody who wants to be associated with it, Hedi Slimane has effectively raised menswear to a credible platform. Men who previously considered fashion a whimsical preoccupation can now confidently show an interest in contemporary menswear. By linking style with music, Dior Homme has become one of the coolest and most sought after brands in modern menswear.

In 2007, Slimane left his position as creative director of Dior Homme after seven years with the brand. Belgian designer Kris Van Assch, who has worked with Slimane, replaced the highly successful designer in this prestigious role. Slimane's reasons for leaving were described on his website: *'I decided to walk away from Dior, and move entirely forward. I had a certain idea of the house of Dior, which I love, and tried to express it through different mediums. It won't be for me to judge if it was of any relevance. I was just trying something.'*

RIGHT: SLIMANE'S AUTUMN/WINTER 05/06 COLLECTION FOR DIOR EXPLORED HIS FASCINATION WITH MUSIC AND ITS STYLE ICONS, SUCH AS PETE DOHERTY, BOBBY GILLESPIE OF PRIMAL SCREAM AND DAVID BOWIE. *OPPOSITE:* CONTEMPORARY DIOR HOMME HAS PRESENTED NEW IDEAS ON MASCULINITY AS HEDI SLIMANE HAS CHANGED THE ACCEPTED PERCEPTIONS OF MODERN MENSWEAR. THE JACKET AND T-SHIRT ARE BOTH FROM THE AUTUMN/WINTER 04/05 COLLECTION.

The true contemporary identity of the Dior brand is attributed to SLIMANE WHO HAS DEVELOPED A DISTINCT IMAGE THAT HAS BEEN STAMPED ON TO NOT JUST CLOTHES but also furnishings, books, photography, fragrances and store design. In an ever-competitive luxury brand market, Dior Homme has managed to DEFINE THE MODERN AESTHETIC and make it desirable to today's male consumer.

DRIES VAN NOTEN

As a legend in his home country, Dries Van Noten is renowned for his GENTLE AND MODERN clothes. WASHED FABRICS, LUXURIOUS CUTS AND A SKILFUL USE OF COLOUR all combine to create clothes that always commemorate wearability. By endorsing the primary pleasure of wearing clothes, Van Noten is the ULTIMATE CLOTHING ENTHUSIAST.

Born in Antwerp, Belgium in 1958, Dries Van Noten came from a family of tailors. His father owned a menswear shop and his grandfather was a traditional tailor. Dries studied at the Antwerp Royal Academy of Fine Arts Fashion Department, from which he graduated in 1980. As a student he worked as a freelance designer for Belgian and Italian labels.

OPPOSITE: FOR HIS AUTUMN/WINTER 07/08 COLLECTION, DRIES VAN NOTEN FUSED VERSACE-LIKE PATTERNS WITH GAUZY ASYMMETRICAL KNITWEAR. PLAYING WITH TEXTURE AND COLOUR IS KEY TO THE SUCCESS OF HIS MENSWEAR GARMENTS. *LEFT:* VAN NOTEN BASED HIS AUTUMN/WINTER 06/07 SHOW ON THREE PRINCIPLES: ELEGANCE, TRADITION AND PROPORTION. HE BELIEVES THAT ALL HIS GARMENTS SHOULD BE INTERCHANGED EASILY, AS IT IS UP TO THE WEARER TO DEFINE THEIR OWN LOOK. *ABOVE:* THE AUTUMN/WINTER 04/05 COLLECTION CELEBRATES SPORTING AND ROMANTIC HEROES, CONJURING UP MEMORIES OF FAR-AWAY TIMES. HIS PRESENTATIONS ALWAYS MERGE THE CLASSIC AND THE CONTEMPORARY TO CREATE A DISTINCT AESTHETIC.

In 1985, *VAN NOTEN* launched his own line and, a year later, he received international acclaim when he presented his men's collection in London and became a member of the 'Antwerp Six'. With his contemporaries Ann Demeulemeester, Walter Van Beirendonck, Dirk Van Saene, Dirk Bikkembergs and Marina Yee, all graduates of the Antwerp Royal Academy, the Belgian designer showed his vision to the international fashion world and placed Antwerp firmly on the fashion map.

Van Noten's menswear collection made such a strong impression that Barney's of New York, Whistles of London and Pauw of Amsterdam placed large orders. Next, Van Noten opened his flagship store, *Het Modepaleis* (The Fashion Palace), in Antwerp in 1989, housed in an elaborate nineteenth-century building. Within a few years, showrooms had opened in Paris, Milan, Tokyo, Hong Kong and many other cities. He has since opened shops in 25 countries, including Tokyo and Hong Kong, and over 500 retailers stock the Dries Van Noten label. Van Noten has a passionate and faithful following of customers, selling over 100,000 pieces each season despite the fact that he does not advertise the label. His company still remains independent, unlike many of his contemporaries.

In 1991, Van Noten first showed his men's collection on the Paris runway, following two years later with his women's collection. He became renowned for his Oriental and African-inspired collections and shows, but it was really the menswear label that established his distinct style. His fascination with fabrics, texture and form classifies the brand. His work is characterized by a creative use of prints (often ethnic), colours, original fabrics and layering.

To celebrate his fiftieth fashion show in 2004, Van Noten presented a show in which models walked along a long dining table. A book entitled *01-50* was also launched to mark the moment.

As a designer who works INTUITIVELY, Van Noten aims to produce desirable, luxurious clothes that are IMMEDIATELY WEARABLE.

He is fascinated by both the design process and the final product and focuses his work on his very strong artistic sensibility and a sharp eye for detail. His clothes are unassuming and even subtle, as his garments always appear easy, natural and sophisticated.

A PAINTERLY AND INNOVATIVE USE OF COLOUR is key to the success of the menswear range, which often incorporates Van Noten's trademark RICH COLOURS. The most EXCLUSIVE FABRICS are used to create his modern garments, which are stylish enough to appeal to a wide male market and contemporary enough to appeal to fashion-forward consumers and also to the influential fashion press and buyers.

Always recognizable, the menswear collections communicate the exotic Van Noten signature and fuse diverse references in a sublime way. His clothes have been described as *'encompassing crossroads of cultures'*. Typical of Van Noten's designs are the extensive use of handcrafting and luxurious, authentic materials, which he buys from suppliers, the names of whom he does not disclose. He designs his garments piece by piece and does not present one distinct theme. Rather, he allows the customer to decide how to put the garments together himself to create his own individual look.

Van Noten's contribution to contemporary menswear lies in his constant ability to produce wearable modern clothes. His philosophy is founded on a solid mastery of the art of tailoring, to which he has added discreet sportswear styling details and cultural references through globally sourced fabrics. Van Noten's distinct personal style manages to be both classical and original; his clothes appeal to those who want to express their individuality rather than follow fickle fashion trends. His collections never seem difficult or too challenging to wear, however, as they always communicate charm and acceptability.

Not so common in the world of fashion, Van Noten has created a brand that successfully balances the commercial and the creative.

VAN NOTEN PRESENTED HIS SPRING/SUMMER 03 SHOW OUTSIDE, NEXT TO THE RIVER SEINE IN PARIS. COMBINING A VARIETY OF TEXTILES, INCLUDING TWEEDS, COTTON AND LINEN, THE BOHEMIAN COLLECTION WAS BOTH TAILORED AND RELAXED.

DUCKIE BROWN

As a transatlantic design team, Duckie Brown has captured a MODERN ATTITUDE TO DRESSING UP. Incorporating a stylish quirkiness with solid tailoring skills, the garments are distinguished by humorous details. As a PURVEYOR OF CHARM, the label has unashamedly pushed male accessories and cheekily juxtaposed unconventional garments with seasonal trendsetters.

New York–based menswear label Duckie Brown consists of Steven Cox and Daniel Silver. The quirky menswear brand is sold through retailers in New York, London, Paris and Japan. The design team was nominated in 2006 for the Council of Fashion Designers of America (CFDA) Perry Ellis New Menswear Award, and they have exhibited their garments at the Victoria & Albert Museum in London. Cox is a former designer at Tommy Hilfiger and Silver is a former daytime TV producer. Between them they have contributed to the eclectic mix of menswear coming out of New York. The name is inspired by Cox's aunt, who called him 'Duckie', and the duo also wanted to add a classic English name, so 'Brown' was chosen.

OPPOSITE: HUMOUR IS KEY TO DUCKIE BROWN'S COLLECTIONS. THE GREY JUMPER WITH EXTRA LONG SLEEVES IS FROM THE SPRING/SUMMER 07 COLLECTION. *BELOW:* BALACLAVAS AND WOOLLY HATS HAVE BECOME A SIGNATURE STYLE FOR DUCKIE BROWN; THIS GREY VERSION IS FROM THE AUTUMN/WINTER 03/04 COLLECTION. THE LABEL USES STRIPES TO MODERNIZE TRADITIONAL TAILORING AS SHOWN ON THIS STRIPY BLAZER FROM THE AUTUMN/WINTER 06/07 COLLECTION.

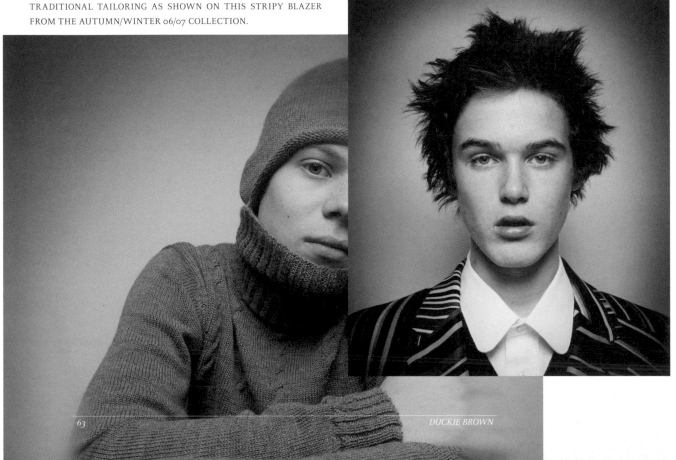

DUCKIE BROWN

The **_DUCKIE BROWN_** aesthetic is characterized by humour and eccentricity. The look is usually bright, sometimes psychedelic, but the shape, cut and fabric are imminently stylish and wearable. The real source of their inspiration, their unique selling point, is their identity as individuals. Cox attributes his design references to a combination of living in the UK for 23 years and in New York for 16 years. For Silver, his aesthetic comes from within. _'It's mine. It comes from me. It's elegant and dishevelled. Think of a schoolboy in a uniform, with a wonky tie.'_

The designers usually start with their own personalities and experiences when they create a collection. _'Every collection is based on the lives we lead and where we travel. We are inspired by the world we live in and everything that surrounds us; everything that happens to us is reflected in our collections.'_ Duckie Brown aspires to dress men beautifully. Their clothes are for men who want to look good and feel comfortable and sexy in what they are wearing. _'But we don't want them to take themselves too seriously,'_ adds Cox.

Duckie Brown's philosophy is concerned with balancing creativity and commercialism. _'We design beautiful tailored clothing for men that is classic. However we are also interested in pushing the boundaries in menswear design.'_ As a financially self-sufficient team and independent from a commercially driven company, Duckie Brown is afforded creative freedom. They have established their own distinctive signature, and customers and buyers continually receive their visions with eagerness. _'We've been really delighted to discover that any man from twenty to eighty is our customer. Steven's father is an electrician and he wears Duckie Brown,'_ explains Silver. _'The advertising guy, the actor, the Wall Street guy, the musician and the fashionista all want Duckie Brown. They all find something that suits them and we love that. We hopefully offer something for everyone.'_

The Duckie Brown duo is personally involved in all the stages of design, enjoying every aspect. For them, each element is vital to a successful collection, from the thought processes and sketches through to the finished product.

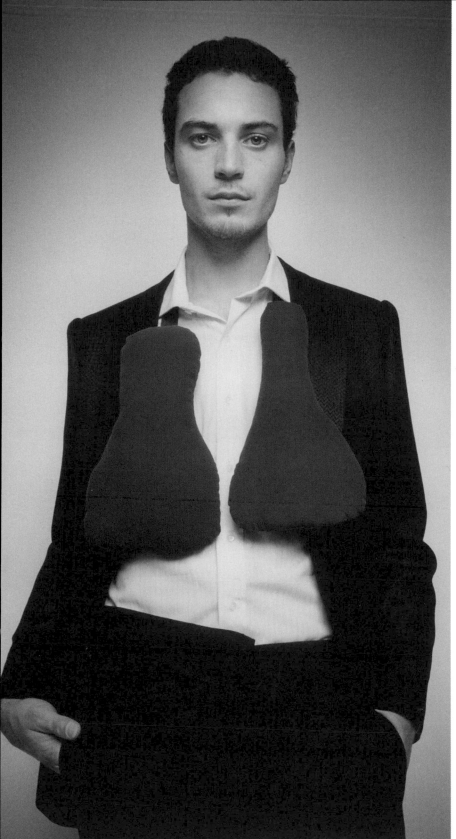

THE ACTUAL DESIGN PROCESS IS DISTINCT. 'We start with
the shoulder and work out. THE CORNERSTONE OF EVERY
COLLECTION IS THE TAILORED JACKET AND TAILORED COAT.
From there, everything comes naturally.' The tailored pieces are
based on tradition, specifically English traditional menswear.

THIS PAGE: A BLUE HOODED KNIT FOR SPRING/SUMMER 05 AND A SKETCH FOR AUTUMN/WINTER 05/06 SHOW DUCKIE BROWN'S APPETITE FOR BOLD COLOURS. *OPPOSITE:* OVERSIZED KNITWEAR, AS IN THIS PIECE FOR AUTUMN/WINTER 06/07, IS ANOTHER CONCEPT THAT DUCKIE BROWN HAS EXPERIMENTED WITH TO BRING WIT TO THEIR COLLECTIONS.

It is not just English tradition that inspires the team. They are frequently informed by everything British, from punk and street wear to royalty. Their vision is European fused with an international understanding of menswear design. Their collections have sometimes been related to the grunge scene, which was promoted in New York and was inspired by 'thrift store' fashion. But Duckie Brown's designs are actually the opposite of the flea-market aesthetic in that they are always high-end luxury collections with contemporary garments made in quality fabrics. Their design icons are Karl Lagerfeld, Rei Kawakubo, Ralph Lauren and Carol Christian Poell. The team experiments with proportion by creating oversized shirts and pants. They successfully design extremes of menswear – the conventional and plain and the avant-garde – but it is through the accessories that Duckie Brown really allows its kookiness to prevail. Usually whimsical and comical, these pieces have included underwear with attached gloves and soft cuddly toys that are worn around the neck.

Duckie Brown presentations always develop fresh ways to show the menswear. Their distinct perspective is personal and is reflected in every collection. Their ability to experiment with fabrics, colours and proportions and, at the same time, push the boundaries is progressive without producing clothing that is unwearable.

Daniel Silver and Steven Cox have been careful to nurture their clients by only increasing sales by a small margin each season. They are very aware that each collection must have the right mix of classic, hand-tailored pieces and more unusual items in order to sell well. The team has ambitions to design a moderately priced collection for men and women, in addition to a high-end women's collection and they are also keen to consult or design for other labels. *'The business of the fashion business is the most difficult aspect of being a designer,'* they explain. *'We believe we are successful because we design clothing we consider to be beautiful, wearable and to have its own signature. We follow our gut and we always follow our hearts.'*

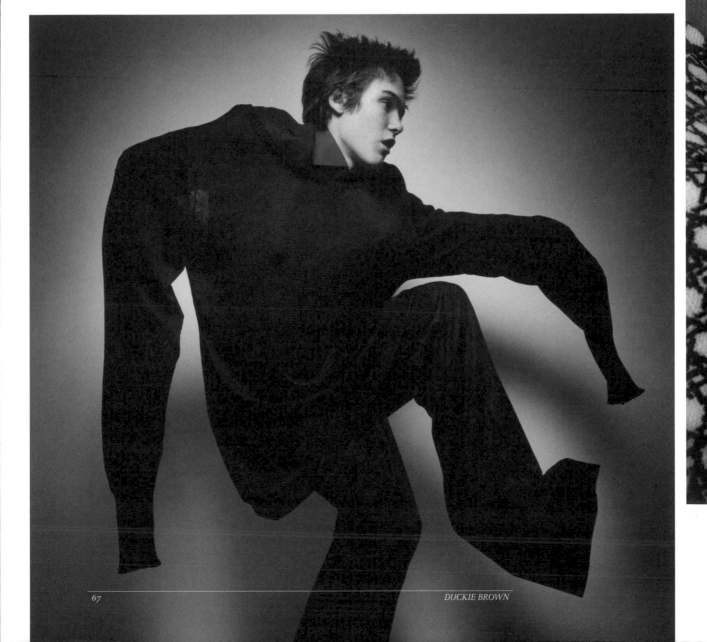

FRANK LEDER

As a champion of German innovation, Frank Leder creates clothes that are characterized by CHARM AND WIT. Always inspired by his home country, Leder has carved a distinct niche in the fashion industry with his well-crafted clothes that are PURPOSEFUL AND SOLID.

Leder's garments are embellished with narratives and lashings of humour, and reflect on the functionality and quality of both simple patterns and work clothes. 'Tradition is at the core of my work and where everything comes from. My challenge is to take that given context and inject it with a modern approach: to come up with garments that are well designed, wearable and interesting to look at.'

OPPOSITE: A PROMOTIONAL IMAGE FOR 'BREAK THAT VICIOUS CIRCLE', THE AUTUMN/WINTER 05/06 COLLECTION. *ABOVE:* PHOTOGRAPHED IN 2004 NEAR THE POLISH BORDER IN GERMANY, THIS HOUSE IS COVERED IN BULLET HOLES FROM THE HOUSE-TO-HOUSE FIGHTING THAT TOOK PLACE DURING WORLD WAR II.

ABOVE: THE PIGEON, WHICH SYMBOLIZES PEACE AND FREEDOM FOR LEDER, IS WEARING A PRINTED FABRIC PRISON SUIT. ACCORDING TO LEDER, 'THE COLLECTION WAS CONCERNED WITH THE IDEA OF BREAKING FREE,' AND LEDER FELT THAT THE USE OF A PIGEON INJECTED HUMOUR AND IRONY.

Born in Nuremberg in Germany, **_FRANK LEDER_** studied fashion design at Central St Martins College in London, where he was awarded an MA with distinction. During his studies, Leder simultaneously worked on his own collection, which he sold to the avant-garde boutique Pineal Eye in Soho, London. Leder also worked as an art director and stylist for fashion magazines *i-D*, *Sleazenation* and *Qvest*.

Leder has been showing his collections in London since 1999, and in 2002 he made his debut at the Paris Menswear Collections. In the same year, he was awarded the Pyramid Award. (In association with Deutsche Bank, the University of the Arts London presents two Pyramid Awards each year – one for fashion and one for photography. The award is intended as a 'springboard' to help a graduating student from each discipline to start up a business or conduct a project in the year after they leave university.) Leder's work has been featured in various gallery exhibitions in Tokyo and Germany, appearing alongside other German fashion designers such as Bernhard Willhelm, Bless, Stephan Schneider and Dirk Schönberger. In 2003, Leder set up a sub-brand, called Raw Power, with business partner Michael Ellis. This label was a T-shirt–based collection created to reach a wider audience.

Taking a humorous and intellectual approach to fashion design, Leder describes it as *'a grounded, down-to-earth thinking with*

an unconventional way of working and perceiving.' Predominantly a concept-driven designer, he is dedicated to creating high-quality garments that recall his native Germany of the past, but retain modernity at their core. *'I create garments that are part of a bigger picture but can settle into a given story,'* explains Leder. *'I design clothes that can reflect a certain intellectual humour in their own context.'*

Leder established himself in London with his impromptu fashion shows in the streets. He was unwilling to adhere to the conventions of British fashion and took his debut collection, 'Let Me Grow', on a series of peaceful demonstrations outside official catwalk presentations. He became known for his individual and progressive way of presenting collections. Through these performances, Leder deals with his position in the fashion industry in an intellectual way, and his work often breaks with the idea of a traditional method of presentation by proposing a different viewpoint. These shows became motifs for Leder's existence within the fashion industry. Various areas would be cordoned off with a red ribbon and Leder's friends would disembark from his white van and present an ad-hoc fashion show on the street. Another event involved a procession of people carrying lanterns bearing his name from Kensington to Battersea in London.

Leder has a specific design process that involves collating images and ideas that filter through his own system. *'My garments settle into a world that is defined by my own photographic aesthetic and artistic fundamentals,'* he says. *'My offerings do not necessarily limit themselves to garments, but grow into areas as diverse as photography and architecture.'*

The garments that Leder designs, therefore, reflect his very personal way of thinking and perceiving. He is driven to see an abstract idea being transformed into a wearable and striking garment. *'A garment is complete, when it settles into my given context of design philosophy and structure. My aim is always to create a garment that can stand by itself and at the same time it settles into and is part of a bigger system.'*

Innovative menswear, according to Leder, should be rooted in a strong design language. It should show its own character and communicate its origin. The identification of the garment is important, as well as a certain aspect of discovery and intellectual stimulation. Leder also maintains that masculinity is integral: *'A trouser is a trouser and should be worn as such.'*

In 2002, Leder returned to Berlin to celebrate his German identity. *'I wanted my clothes to be a product of my very own design environment,'* he explains. His garments appeal to consumers who value his very strong and defined aesthetic. Leder describes them as *'Every person who wants to walk a certain route and path with me and my offerings. Those who want to open a new door and are prepared to discover.'*

OPPOSITE: GERMAN PAINTER MARTIN EDER WEARS LEDER'S AFRIKA COLLECTION FROM SPRING/SUMMER 07. ***ABOVE:*** A CORNER OF LEDER'S DESIGN STUDIO HAS THE DISTINCT UTILITARIAN AESTHETIC THAT IS ALSO EVIDENT IN HIS CLOTHES.

Leder believes strongly in producing contemporary clothes. His garments may be ROOTED IN THE PAST but they are essentially modern in their WEARABILITY AND APPROACH. His unique design philosophy and desire to follow a different path in the presentation of his garments may be distinctly German. Whether staging a show for blind people or inviting buyers and press to view his new collection in his father's hometown in Bohemia, LEDER SUCCESSFULLY PRESENTS A VERY PERSONAL VISION. In combining a mischievous curiosity with a nod to tradition and a HEALTHY SENSE OF HUMOUR, Leder has created his very own niche in contemporary fashion.

OPPOSITE: THE 'SPY READING NEWSPAPER' WAS A PROJECT CREATED IN 2003 WITH PHOTOGRAPHER GREGOR HOHENBERG. THE SERIES WAS PUBLISHED IN SPRING 2004 IN *INTERSECTION* MAGAZINE. THE COAT IS FROM THE SPRING/SUMMER 03 COLLECTION. *ABOVE:* 'THE ARCHITECT' WAS ANOTHER PROJECT LEDER UNDERTOOK WITH PHOTOGRAPHER GREGOR HOHENBERG IN 2005, USING LEDER'S AUTUMN/ WINTER 04/05 CLOTHES. AGAIN, A NARRATIVE AND CHARACTERS ARE USED TO COMMUNICATE LEDER'S GARMENTS; LEDER HIMSELF APPEARS AS THE ARCHITECT WITH BLUEPRINTS UNDER HIS ARM.

GASPARD YURKIEVICH

CONVENTIONAL RULES OF MASCULINITY ARE QUESTIONED by Gaspard Yurkievich, who often experiments with male sexuality during his fashion presentations. Designing INVENTIVE AND ALTERNATIVE FORMS OF DRESS is integral to Yurkievich's philosophy. Fusing French tradition with a youthful approach, his collections always have an edge.

Gaspard Yurkievich is at the cutting edge of a new generation of French designers, and his work often explores sexuality and historic references. He developed his menswear collection after several successful years of showing womenswear. 'There is no difference of vision between the contemporary menswear and womenswear. I like it when there is a connection with the body and spirit, a vision that is best described as conceptually sexy.'

OPPOSITE: ENTITLED 'I THINK L'AMOUR IS COMING BACK', THE AUTUMN/WINTER 06/07 COLLECTION INVOLVED MODELS BEING SUBSTITUTED WITH PERFORMERS TO CREATE A MORE CONTEMPORARY APPROACH TO THE TRADITIONAL CATWALK SHOW. **LEFT:** A BACKSTAGE IMAGE OF A MODEL AT THE AUTUMN/ WINTER 07/08 SHOW AT THE CENTRE POMPIDOU IN PARIS. YURKIEVICH ALWAYS CHOOSES MODELS WHO REFLECT THE AESTHETIC OF THE COLLECTION.

Born in Paris in 1972 to French–Argentine parents, _YURKIEVICH_ studied at the fashion school Studio Berçot in Paris from 1991 to 1993. He worked for Thierry Mugler in 1992, Jean-Paul Gaultier in 1993 and went on to assist Jean Colonna in 1994. These varied jobs provided Yurkevich with a diverse experience of French fashion design.

Between 1996 and 1998, he took part in three consecutive fashion competitions. The first was the Young Designers Fashion Show of the Senken Shimbun in Tokyo in 1996, and the second was the 12th International Festival of the Arts and Fashion at Hyères in the south of France in 1997. Hyères marked Yurkievich's breakthrough in fashion as he was awarded both the renowned womenswear prize and the 3 Suisses prize. Thirdly, in 1998, he won France's ANDAM (National Association for the Development of Fashion Arts) competition, the prize for which was funds to help him produce his next collection.

Yurkievich then founded his own label, and presented his first prêt-à-porter collection 'Distressed' for the Autumn/Winter season 99/00 in Paris. The following year Yurkievich created collections for one of the largest mail-order houses in the world, La Redoute, and for the French retailer Monoprix. As well as his regular presentations, he also participated in various fashion events such as the 'French Fashion Furor 2000' in Singapore along with such other labels as Jerome Dreyfuss, Isabelle Ballu, Tom van Lingen and Christian Dior. He also staged fashion shows in New York, Zurich, Tokyo and São Paolo in 1999.

Since 1998, Yurkievich has been showing his womenswear collections during Paris Fashion Week. His first menswear collection, entitled 'Pornography', debuted in Paris in June 2003, in which he dressed four male professional dancers as an alternative to traditional male models. _'For our menswear collection, the first concern is masculinity. It is very important because we launched the menswear after five years of designing womenswear, which was very feminine and sophisticated. It was key not to create any confusion between the two collections. The men's collections are clearly more casual, but are now gradually becoming more and more sophisticated.'_

In his catwalk shows, Yurkievich is interested in the location, setting and scenography. Original soundtracks are created by musicians to enhance the experience for the audience. Fashion communicators are Yurkievich's inspiration, such as stylist Ray Petri and photographer Bruce Weber.

DANCERS AT THE CENTRE POMPIDOU IN PARIS PERFORMED THE PRESENTATION FOR YURKIEVICH'S 'BIG FUN' COLLECTION FROM SPRING/SUMMER 05.

GASPARD YURKIEVICH

BACKSTAGE IMAGES FROM YURKIEVICH'S AUTUMN/WINTER 07/08 COLLECTION.

THE DESIGN PROCESS IS METHODICAL. 'It usually follows the same route,' Yurkievich states. 'Sometimes a very strong mood will appear to us as an evident item to follow, but an intuitive approach to a more CONCRETE AND ELABORATE VISION is a constant in the process.'

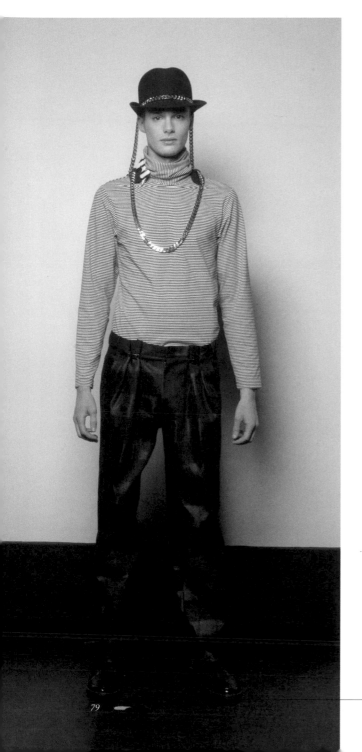

Yurkievich sees his work as an ever-evolving process that encompasses his immediate team. *'For the men's collection I work closely with my partner Guido and we react on the last collection and we have discussions every day. The design process is very intuitive and then becomes more and more constructed.'*

All the menswear collections suggest alternatives for modern men. His intention is to design innovative and modern clothes. *'My customers are the same generation as me and they want to look sophisticated. They are people looking for an alternative to just tailoring and sportswear.'*

Traditional tailoring is not the focus of Yurkievich's menswear collections. *'It's more about how to style the basics, which I consider as a second skin, and then new elements come to build a new proposition.'* This concept of challenging basic garment types allows Yurkievich's clothes to become progressive and alternative. The cloth, therefore, is a focal point at the beginning of a collection. *'I enjoy working on fabrics, and seeing the clothes becoming real in the atelier is very rewarding.'*

Design experimentation is vital in Yurkievich's creative journey. *'I am very versatile when designing my menswear. I need my clothes to follow my mood, and some days we feel powerful and sometimes we just want to be invisible. That's why our collections turn basics into more extreme pieces.'*

Yurkievich's menswear is distinctly urban and modern. Breaking away from the Parisian tradition of conformity, Yurkievich hopes that his collections communicate with a contemporary and forward-thinking clientele. *'I think I look for all kinds of emotions when I make clothes,'* explains Yurkievich. *'The thing that moves me is nostalgia; it's not about being reactionary or obsessed with the past; it's about being optimistic.'*

'THE BIG WET SHINY BOOBIES' COLLECTION FOR SPRING/SUMMER 07 ILLUSTRATED VIBSKOV'S INDIVIDUAL AND HUMOROUS APPROACH TO THE PRESENTATION OF HIS CLOTHES. HE DESCRIBED THE COLLECTION AS 'VERY PLAYGROUND AND A BIT ASEXUAL', ADHERING TO HIS DESIGN SIGNATURE OF CREATING QUIRKY, FUN AND COLOURFUL CLOTHES.

HENRIK VIBSKOV

Working as a DESIGNER, FILM-MAKER, MUSICIAN AND ARTIST, Henrik Vibskov brings a multifaceted perspective to fashion. His work combines HUMOUR, CRAFTSMANSHIP and an extraordinary ATTENTION TO DETAIL. Tailored for a perfect fit, Vibskov's clothes, like his visionary fashion presentations, NEVER FAIL TO ENTERTAIN.

The first Dane to be represented on the Paris catwalks, Henrik Vibskov brings a multi-disciplinary approach to the fashion industry. Vibskov was born in 1972, and grew up in the countryside of Jutland in Denmark. Constantly pushing his creative boundaries, he is fuelled by a feverish interest in fashion, film and music.

HENRIK VIBSKOV

Before entering the world of fashion, _VIBSKOV_ was motivated by music. Winning a break-dance competition at the age of 12 furthered his fascination with the dance floor. Vibskov's drumming, often played live on the streets of Europe, has been featured on eight releases with international artists. He has also played on the radio and worked with the Danish Grammy winner Marie Frank.

Moving on from music, Vibskov worked as a creative in the visual arts, encompassing both film and music. Exhibitions in cult spaces, including the Midwest Gallery in Tokyo, the Millbank Gallery in London, Sotheby's Gallery in New York and V1 Gallery in Copenhagen, have all presented his very graphic work. In 1996, Vibskov was a finalist in the Smirnoff International Fashion Awards, and from this success he went to work for established Danish fashion label Bruuns Bazaar.

In 2000, Vibskov, along with fellow Danish film-maker Thomas Jessen, won the prestigious Beck's Futures first prize for the film _The Monk_. The following year another film by Vibskov, entitled _The Egg_, was also shortlisted for the award.

After studying at the Hillevi Van Deurs Design School in Copenhagen, Denmark, Vibskov decided to challenge his fashion ideology and he enrolled at Central St Martins College in London in 1998. He graduated in 2001 and received a vast amount of media interest from style magazines around the world. _i-D_, _The Face, Brutus, Dazed & Confused, Wallpaper*, Vogue_ and _The New York Times_ all jumped on the Vibskov bandwagon to support the Danish designer.

Presented as a fashion hero in Denmark, Vibskov allowed Danish national television channel DR2 to document his graduation from Central St Martins over a six-week period in 2001. The channel also followed him through the season 03/04. Encouraged by the exposure, Vibskov set up his own-name label, which he has been running since 2000 from his base in Copenhagen.

At the launch of his menswear collection, Vibskov was picked up by a number of trendsetting stores such as Colette in Paris, Pineal Eye in London, Midwest in Tokyo and Traffik in Moscow. Vibskov is a regular at Men's Fashion Week in Paris, where he is known for his innovative, colourful and eclectic menswear.

The Autumn/Winter 04/05 collection was shown in Lucerne, Switzerland, and he was picked for the Swiss Fashion Awards, together with fellow visionary designers Raf Simons and Bernhard Willhelm.

Vibskov's designs question existing shapes in menswear whilst at the same time referencing traditional tailoring. Adding new shapes in innovative colour combinations, he aims to capture the European fashion scene, as well as the lucrative Japanese market.

CONTEMPORARY SILHOUETTES COUPLED WITH BOLD PRINTS AND TEXTURES DEFINE VIBSKOV'S EDGY APPROACH TO MENSWEAR. THE AUTUMN/WINTER 06/07 COLLECTION EXPLORES FAIRYTALES, WITH PSYCHEDELIC-COLOURED PRINTS ON T-SHIRTS AND JACKETS, JESTER-STYLE LEGGINGS AND CHERRY-RED SUITS.

'I work very intuitively and my design reflects my personality,' explains Vibskov, whose early musical triumphs still have an influence on his concepts. 'I do what I need for myself basically. I play drums, for instance, and so I made shorts with leather inserts, where I could hold the drums. I guess my view on life is very laid back in a way, and I would like to make things that make people smile.'

The process of design is constantly stimulating, Vibskov believes. 'The ideas make new ideas, which make new ideas. It never stops but sometimes you have to stop otherwise it can be pretty annoying.' His design practice is a reflection of his contemporary and edgy clothes. 'Sometimes it starts off in the same track, then I jump on a new bus, maybe fall asleep and wake up, go back a little, jump off, take a new bus, sit on the front seat, have a chat with the driver, maybe a sandwich, jump off, walk a little, then suddenly a fast bus, a wow-wow design process has to be finished.'

Successful menswear, according to Vibskov, is a combination of creative, sales and personal perspectives, all of which are integral to each other. 'I often do a collection and then I mix it up completely again two days before the show in Paris. Then I might make some other new garments the night before. Last minute is my thing and the feeling of chaos usually ensures a good vibe. I hope so anyway.'

This design method relies on a very personal sense of intuition. He finds immense worth in creating and changing his ideas instantly. 'I very much like the concept from jazz music of a jam session,' he explains. 'You can, in a second, twist the whole feeling and energy of a song. You can't do this in fashion with the same quickness. Fashion can be a bit long-winded in another way, because of the deadline thing. If you had to do a new record every half year, it would be crazy.'

Like his contemporaries, Vibskov believes modern menswear is based on an appreciation of tradition that is updated for a modern market. 'I am not afraid of pink for men, but I like the classics like suits and shirts. I am not so much into unisex, as my women's line looks completely different.'

Vibskov feels that the current menswear market is static, but he is respectful of contemporary labels such as Cosmic Wonder and Comme des Garçons. Like them, Vibskov identifies the difficulties of creating modern but wearable fashion. He appreciates the challenge in making his clothes work in a real daily environment and not just allowing them to be concerned with a fantasy world. Vibskov may proclaim that he designs his clothes for his own practical requirements, but he accepts that the real pleasure is when consumers relate to products. 'Hopefully my customer will be wearing my knitted hats with a lovely smile.'

HENRIK VIBSKOV

ABOVE: FOR HIS SPRING/SUMMER 05 COLLECTION, GALLIANO CELEBRATED BAD BOYS BY EXPLORING THE WARDROBES OF BUCCANEERS, GIGOLOS, GYPSIES, TOREADORS, BOXERS AND PIRATES. THE PRESENTATION WAS TRUE TO GALLIANO'S SKILLS IN DRAMATIC SHOWMANSHIP, AS THE STAGE BECAME A VEHICLE FOR A VISUAL DECADENCE AND FANTASY. *OPPOSITE:* RESEARCH IMAGERY USED BY GALLIANO TO DEVELOP CONCEPTS FOR HIS COLLECTIONS.

JOHN GALLIANO

JOHN GALLIANO IS A RADICAL FASHION DESIGNER whose menswear collections continually challenge the contemporary style barometer. With an EXCEPTIONAL TALENT to translate eclectic historical references into fiercely modern clothes, Galliano begs the fashion industry to question traditional menswear. DECADENCE AND FANTASY ARE INTEGRAL to Galliano's world and his visionary shows excite and confront masculinity in fashion.

The upper echelons of fashion royalty rank John Galliano among their number. Infamous for challenging ideologies of clothing, Galliano has created menswear collections that are renowned for their radical vision. It was 2003 that saw the launch of Galliano's menswear line, and in January 2004 he presented his first men's fashion show in Paris. 'With this first collection we had to establish the identity of the brand and decide who the Galliano man is,' he explains. 'He is someone who is romantic, poetic and a bit of a gipsy. He is really a reflection of me.' The concept was an extension of his womenswear label, but Galliano wanted to present a masculine sensibility. 'It's a bit like being in a gentleman's club where you wear very conservative clothes, but on the back of a tie there hides a pin-up image.'

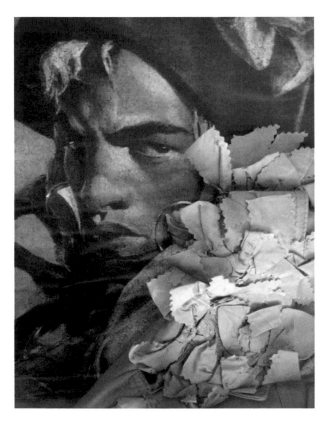

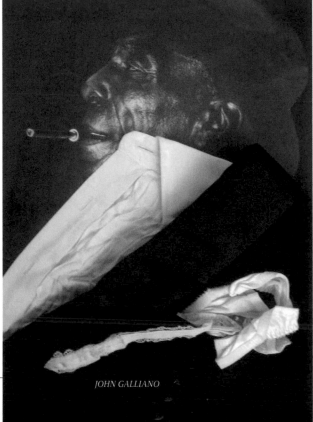

JOHN GALLIANO

GALLIANO'S RESEARCH BOOKS FOR HIS MENSWEAR COLLECTIONS BRING TOGETHER FABRICS, PHOTOGRAPHY AND HISTORICAL RESEARCH. SPANNING MANY CULTURES AND PERIODS, THESE SKETCHBOOKS COMMUNICATE THE ESSENCE OF GALLIANO'S CREATIVE PROCESS.

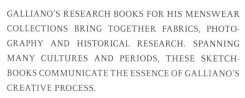

JOHN GALLIANO'S menswear challenges the traditional notion of dress codes. He is enthused by using unconventional fabrics usually associated with womenswear, describing how, *'through the details we use some of the womenswear lingerie vocabulary'.* These details are very subtle, ranging from garter straps on inside pockets to frilly lace on the back of the neckline or from hook and eyes on lapels to corsetry on sleeves. Though always hidden, these motifs support Galliano's concept of creating beautiful clothes from which the wearer can find individual pleasure.

For Galliano, his garments work as a form of escapism. *'It's like giving men a bit of what they've seen on women without taking away their masculinity, allowing them to dream more,'* he explained on the launch of his menswear.

Having already made the bias cut a signature in his womenswear collections, Galliano was the first to translate it into his men's garments. *'It's almost like deconstructing a tailored suit, but without going all the way to sportswear. You've got a formality and the look of a suit, but it's as light as one of our dresses and you feel as if you're wearing a tracksuit. I like funky sportswear and funky tailoring. I do wear suits but I like to mix and match my clothes.'*

Linking sportswear and formal wear is another key element for Galliano. His menswear collections are always a heady and eclectic mix of influences and ideas that reflect his very personal design process. Galliano is a master of research and he spends much of his time feverishly sourcing ideas from around the world for his collections. He may be inspired by a colour, texture, image or anything that he finds stimulating. A story then slowly develops, and that results in a final collection.

Galliano's fashion shows are famous for their elaborate narratives on his current influences and fascinations. For Spring/Summer 06, Galliano was influenced by an array of musicians and buskers – to communicate this the catwalk presentation was based on a musical parade. Galliano was inspired by Bob Dylan from his Woodstock days, playing on stage, with a flower in his hat. Pinstriped suits were customized with silk scarves cut to form musical notes. *'After the concert is finished he's rushed into his limo still wearing his backstage silk pyjamas and his velvet overcoat,'* Galliano muses. Finally, the presentation returned to London, this time to Oxford Street and a procession of Hindu performers with army-surplus jackets and draped combat tunic trousers. The catwalk procession finished with a psychedelic celebration on the beaches of Thailand.

The Autumn/Winter 06/07 collection was described as *'Oliver Twist meets Gorillaz'*; Galliano's imagination never ceases to stimulate. The collection was inspired by Roman Polanski's film adaptation of *Oliver Twist*, interspersed with the cartoon characters from Damon Albarn and Jamie Hewlett's Gorillaz videos. A fascinating voyage ensued, from the nineteenth to the twenty-first century.

Galliano is focused on UNITING TRADITION AND HISTORY WITH CONTEMPORARY INNOVATION. After a visit to fabric factories in Lyons, France, which preserve ancient ways of making cloth, Galliano decided to research new fabric treatments, with the idea of reconciling the old and the new, the ancient and the modern, THE SAVAGE AND THE REFINED.

BELOW: GALLIANO COLLECTIONS ARE ALWAYS A HEADY MIX OF COLOUR, TEXTURE, PATTERN AND SHAPE, AND THE RESULT IS ALWAYS THEATRICAL. HIS PRESENTATIONS ARE AS EXTRAVAGANT AS THE CLOTHES HE DESIGNS; THE SET DESIGN AND LOCATION TAKE THE AUDIENCE INTO GALLIANO'S FANTASTICAL WORLD. THIS IMAGE IS FROM THE SPRING/SUMMER 05 COLLECTION. *OPPOSITE:* FOR HIS AUTUMN/WINTER 05/06 COLLECTION, GALLIANO DREW ON A FAR-REACHING RANGE OF INSPIRATIONS AND INFLUENCES: NAPOLEON, KURT COBAIN, TIBETAN WARRIORS, ELVIS AND HIP HOP WERE ALL PUT IN THE CREATIVE MIX TO CREATE A COLLECTION THAT WAS A VISUAL SPECTACLE.

Thick denims were dusted, waxed or lacquered, suit fabrics were woven with thin metal threads and then washed to create a distinct look. Knits were printed and coats were made of many layers of georgette fabric.

Before Galliano became a contemporary menswear modernist, he had spent many years as a revolutionary in womenswear. Born in 1960 in Gibraltar, Juan Carlos Antonio Galliano moved with his family to London in 1966. Galliano studied fashion at Central St Martins College in London, and his graduation collection in 1984, entitled 'Les Incroyables', was inspired by the French Revolution. The collection was received with immense excitement by both buyers and the press. Joan Burstein of Browns immediately bought the collection, placed it in the window of her boutique, and catapulted both the collection and Galliano into the spotlight.

Galliano continued to show in London until 1992, after which he moved to Paris to present his collections to an international audience. He won the prestigious British Designer of the Year Award in 1988, 1994, 1995 and 1997 (the latter with Alexander McQueen). In 1995, it was announced that Galliano would be the new designer for the house of Givenchy, and two seasons later he took the position of designer for the house of Christian Dior.

In November 2001, John Galliano was presented with a CBE by Queen Elizabeth II. In May 2003, he opened his first boutique in Paris on rue Saint Honoré. *'Hi-tech romance'* is how he described the concept. The shop represents a mix of savagery and refinement; it is raw and polished, contemporary and historical – all ideas that reflect the Galliano design philosophy.

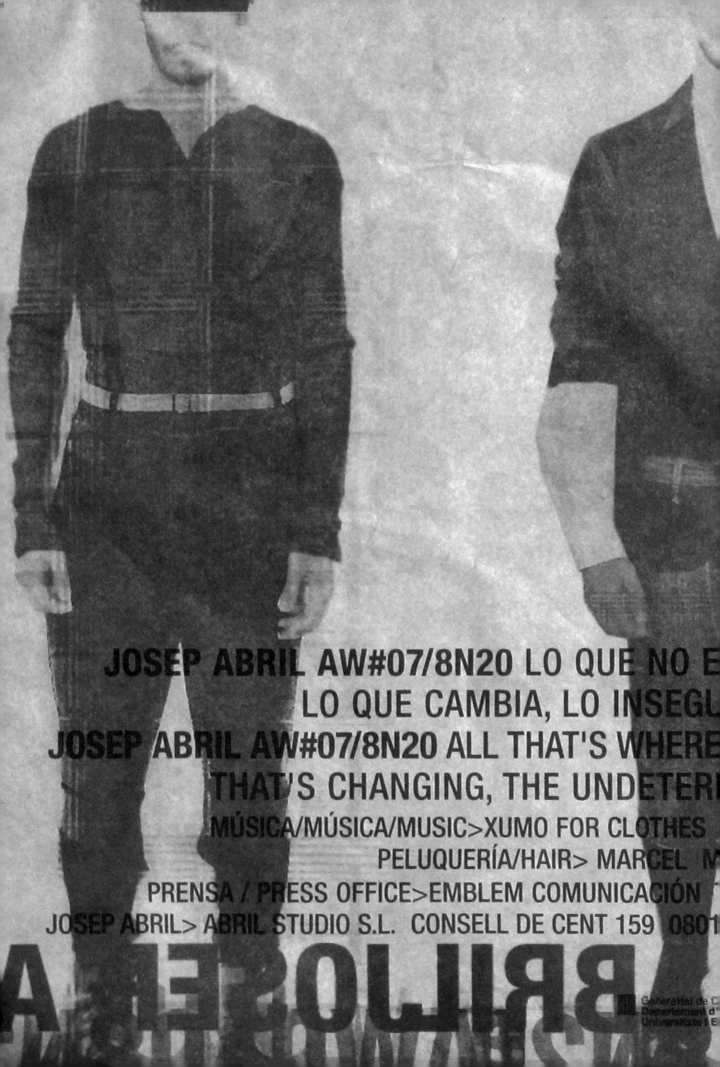

JOSEP ABRIL

The clothes of Spanish designer Josep Abril tend to EXPRESS A DARK SOBRIETY. His work aims to FILL THE VOID OF BLAND CLOTHING by communicating with his customers both physically and emotionally. His clothes, although visually simple, once stripped back reveal a VIGOROUS ATTENTION TO DETAIL.

Inspired by his native Barcelona, Abril is truly a product of his environment. He has exhibited his understated menswear at the Gaudí Catwalk Shows since 1991. Noted for his directional collections, Abril is associated with the group of contemporary European designers based in Barcelona, including Spastor, who are promoting Spanish fashion globally.

OPPOSITE: THE INVITATION TO THE JOSEP ABRIL AUTUMN/WINTER 07/08 SHOW. **THIS PAGE:** IMAGES TAKEN BACK STAGE AT THE AUTUMN/WINTER 05/06 SHOW. ABRIL'S DESIGN AESTHETIC STUDIES THE 'FLIP SIDE' OF EVERYTHING AND THIS INFORMS BOTH HIS FABRIC AND COLOUR CHOICES.

JOSEP ABRIL

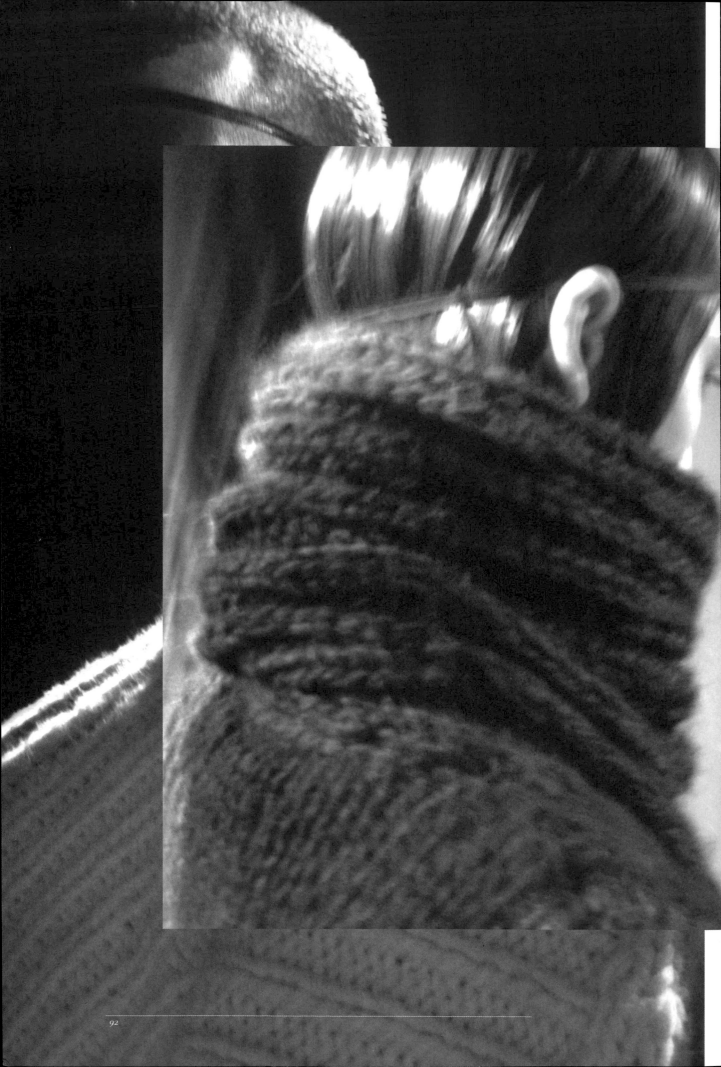

Having studied fine art and fashion in Barcelona, _ABRIL_ won the Gaudí prize for new designers in 1991. In 1996, he presented his first catwalk fashion show in Barcelona and began selling internationally over the next two years. As well as creating collections under his own name, Abril has also designed menswear for Spanish label Armand Basi, a job that won him designer of the year for Spain in 2003. Abril also produces costumes for theatre, dance and performance and, in 2004, he won the _GQ_ award for best menswear designer.

Abril has a succinct design philosophy. _'The beginning is an idea and the end is the clothing. I don't want the process to detract from the origin, but rather to feed it. I look for the "flip side" of everything, my mistakes, the left over and chance.'_ He describes his aesthetic as, _'A wabi-sabi version of my reality, soaked in European tradition.'_ By this he means that he follows the Japanese concept of a simple aesthetic that is pared down to its barest essence. 'Wabi-sabi' is the art of finding beauty in imperfection and profundity in nature. Like many of his contemporaries, Abril is respectful of traditional menswear design but adds his contemporary approach. His distinct and sharp colour palette of mainly black and white runs through all his collections.

'The most fulfilling part of design is when you find direction and follow it, be it a fabric a shape or a technique,' explains Abril who sees the true worth of designing in the reality of a garment. He believes it is difficult to define the customer who wears his clothes, maintaining that he could be anybody who sees an item of clothing and wants it or needs it. His hope is that his customers are complicit and not indifferent to the reasons why they purchase the garments. When customers take Abril's clothes and make them their own by wearing them in an individual way it is very exciting for the designer.

The creative process is seen by Abril as an extension of himself. _'My life is inextricably linked to my work. My attitudes to life, my ideas about the world, what's happening in it and how I feel about it are all reflected in my collections.'_ His design process follows the same method. _'I follow an indispensable methodology so that ideas and intuitions do not get lost and are able to come to fruition, which also allows a certain continuity to the collections.'_

According to Abril, clothes should not be a disguise. _'They should affirm your attitudes and work in harmony with you and with the world in which you live,'_ he explains. He also believes that designers should not be overtly concerned with masculinity when designing menswear. _'It's something that's never concerned me. The line between masculine and feminine is in continuous flux.'_

The most challenging aspect of the design process is finding the essential shape and material to describe his ideas. 'I LIKE TRADITIONAL MATERIALS AND BELIEVE THEY, LIKE US, HAVE A CELLULAR MEMORY, THUS GIVING BOTH PHYSICAL AND EMOTIONAL COMFORT,' _he says._

Abril is very clear when talking about the designers who have inspired him. _'The white of Martin Margiela and the black of Yohji Yamamoto,'_ he states. The influence of these designers' aesthetics is evident in his collections, but Abril presents his own, distinct look. He believes fashion should be concerned with the future and not the past. He does not like to reference previous decades in his designs and avoids any notion of nostalgia.

'In contemporary menswear, man is constantly struggling with what he wants and what he believes he can have. In the market there is always an excess of what the public feels it wants to consume.' To be innovational and modern in his design context is a constant challenge to Abril and he believes the best way to do it is by _'questioning everything, taking nothing for granted, and exploiting the infinite possibilities in things'._

OPPOSITE: A HAND-KNITTED JUMPER FROM THE AUTUMN/WINTER 07/08 COLLECTION COMMUNICATES ABRIL'S DESIRE TO CREATE LUXURIOUS BUT INDIVIDUALLY MADE AND CAREFULLY CONSTRUCTED GARMENTS. _BELOW:_ FOR HIS AUTUMN/WINTER 07/08 SHOW, ABRIL USED KNITTED SOCKS WITH SOLES AS AN ALTERNATIVE TO SHOES.

SKETCHBOOKS SHOWING THE RESEARCH
AND DESIGN DEVELOPMENT FOR ABRIL'S
AUTUMN/WINTER 07/08 COLLECTION.

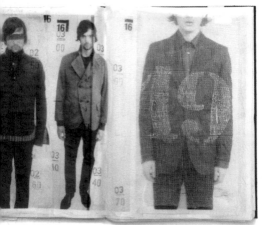

AN OUTFIT FROM THE 'PIEL DE ORO' JOSEP ABRIL SPRING/SUMMER 06 COLLECTION.

KIM JONES

An unassuming innovator of contemporary fashion design, Kim Jones celebrates YOUTH AND COLOUR in his collections. His look is described as high-end casual wear that represents the NEW WAVE OF BRITISH MENSWEAR DESIGN. His clothes span global references and are unified with a London design perspective.

British fashion designer Kim Jones originally studied illustration and then entered Central St Martins College, where he captured the zeitgeist of the time through his contemporary vision for menswear design. Since graduating with an MA in menswear in 2002, Jones has developed a cult following due to his distinctive bright, casual and slouchy clothing. He is credited with having encouraged a resurgence of interest in contemporary casual clothing in British menswear design.

OPPOSITE: FOR HIS AUTUMN/WINTER 05/06 COLLECTION, KIM JONES DESIGNED CASUAL GARMENTS THAT USED SPORTSWEAR DETAILING. THE SLOUCHY RELAXED STYLE IS TYPICAL OF JONES'S CLOTHES. THE IMAGE IS TAKEN FROM *DOINGBIRD MAGAZINE,* ISSUE 9, STYLING BY JOE MCKENNA AND PHOTOGRAPHY BY ALASDAIR MCLELLAN. *ABOVE:* AN INVITATION TO THE SPRING/ SUMMER 07 FASHION SHOW, ENTITLED 'AFRICA'.

JONES'S debut collection 'Music Box' took inspiration from the Chicago club of the same name. Brightly coloured, unpretentious street wear became the aesthetic that propelled Jones's work to international acclaim. Having spent most of his youth travelling with his family, Jones has soaked up street culture from all over the world and channelled it into his relaxed and easy solutions for contemporary clothing.

As well as designing his own collection, Jones has worked for Mulberry, Hugo Boss and Umbro. He has created a 15-piece collection for Topman, which quickly sold out, and has also worked on a design project for vodka company Absolut, which featured his shot glasses in Swedish hotels. Jones has worked as an art director and stylist for publications *Dazed & Confused, Numero Homme, Another Magazine, 10* and *The New York Times*. In 2004, *The Face* magazine described him as number 20 in the top 100 influential people in fashion. *GQ* magazine has nominated him three times for the Man of the Year Award, and Jones has received three nominations at the UK *Elle* Style Awards.

Musician Jo Reynolds and accessories designer Sally Turner collaborated with Jones on jewelry and accessories for his early catwalk shows. He received Topshop New Generation sponsorship for his London Fashion Week debut in 2002, which included womenswear, and he won this award again in 2003, becoming the first menswear designer to do so.

Sportswear has always been fundamental to Jones's design philosophy, but his signature has further developed to use both sportswear and tailoring. Although his collections look effortless and sometimes experimental, they are always constructed using a sophisticated knowledge of the formal methods of tailoring. By twisting athletic wear with formal wear, Jones makes clothes that are inherently modern. He collaborates on part of his collection with tailor Timothy Everest to emphasize the importance of tailoring. Although he says that this is not the focus of his collection, tailoring does allow Jones to present sharp and precise clothes.

Jones's fashion presentations are progressive and varied, and are defined by his individual choice of models, which he often scouts off the street. He has created films with fashion photographer Toyin and a book with American art photographer Luke Smalley. His work was featured in 'The London Look – Fashion from Street to Catwalk' exhibition at the Museum of London in 2004–05.

In September 2003, Jones showed his first catwalk collection at London Fashion Week. In 2004, he debuted his collection at the Paris Men's Fashion Week and, in 2007, he crossed the Atlantic to present his collection to buyers and press in New York. For this collection, Jones explored technology-enhanced fabrics on sportswear shapes, which he has developed since to become a signature of his work. Working with Savile Row tailors Norton & Sons, he used new luxury materials, such as shearling and baby alpaca, to create sportswear shapes. He changed basic active-wear garments by altering their proportion. A baseball jacket was made coat length and denim tracksuit pants were reworked with multi-pleats.

The CELEBRATION OF YOUTH CULTURE has been integral to the establishment of the Jones aesthetic. Described sometimes as portraying YOUTHFUL EROTICISM, Jones's fashion shows often use young boys as models. Jones maintains that he is not playing with sexual identities, but instead he sees these individuals as INSPIRATION for his collections. In other words, he presents characters that he feels should wear his clothes.

The early collections evolved from bright sportswear-focused garments to urban and modern clothes that appeal to a youthful generation. Jones's clothes are distinct and attract customers who want directional but not difficult clothes. His significant contribution to men's fashion is his ability to produce forward-thinking garments that are void of ambiguity and pretension. His clothes are essentially young, bright and wearable.

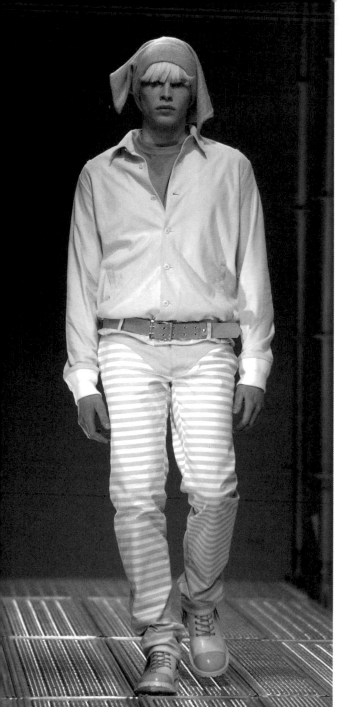

OPPOSITE: DRAWING FOR AN EMBROIDERY DESIGN IN THE AUTUMN/ WINTER 07/08 COLLECTION. *ABOVE:* FOR HIS AUTUMN/WINTER 05/06 COLLECTION, JONES WAS INSPIRED BY RUSSIAN PRISONERS AND THE 1980S LONDON LABEL BODY MAP. *TOP RIGHT:* KIM JONES'S STUDIO DURING THE PLANNING OF THE SPRING/SUMMER 08 COLLECTION. *RIGHT:* IN THE AUTUMN/WINTER 06/07 COLLECTION, KIM JONES COLLABORATED WITH LONDON TAILOR TIMOTHY EVEREST, RESULTING IN A MORE FORMAL-FOCUSED PRESENTATION. A HUGE INFLATABLE RABBIT AND ELEPHANT WERE PLACED ON THE CATWALK TO REFERENCE JEFF KOONS'S POP ART.

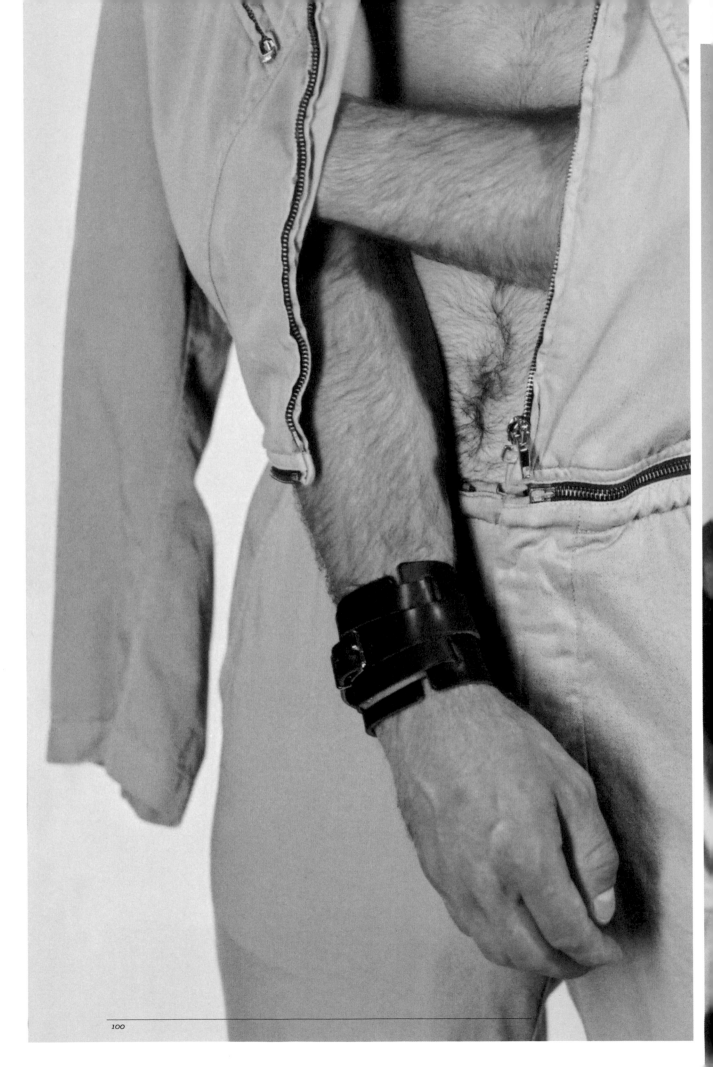

MAISON MARTIN MARGIELA

The fashion industry's favourite philosopher Martin Margiela keeps a low profile at the helm of Maison Martin Margiela. His garments are characterized by an APPRECIATION OF IMPERFECTION, PERSONALITY AND ECCENTRICITY. Collections are presented on tube platforms and street corners, as the extremities and changes of daily life inform his academic concepts. Margiela's artisan aesthetic has come to define modernity with intelligent and covetable clothes.

Radical creative Martin Margiela is infamously described as the fashion designer's fashion designer. He is elusive and only responds to interviews via fax and under the guise of 'Maison Martin Margiela'. The label has become a cult with the mysterious designer as its leader. He is never photographed or interviewed personally. Even the labels on his clothes remain blank with a simple number circled to classify the collection. Menswear is number 10.

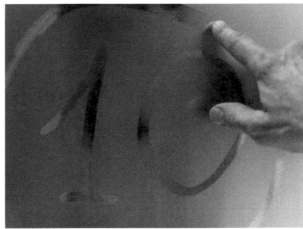

OPPOSITE: A LEATHER ARMBAND CONFORMS TO THE MINIMALIST ARTISAN QUALITY THAT DEFINES THIS CONCEPTUAL DESIGNER. THE PIECE IS FROM THE SPRING/SUMMER 02 COLLECTION. *LEFT:* A WHITE SHIRT WITH 'WHITE' WRITTEN IN REVERSE IS TYPICAL OF MAISON MARTIN MARGIELA'S PLAY ON WORDS AND LANGUAGE. THE IMAGE IS FROM PROMOTIONAL MATERIAL FOR THE SPRING/ SUMMER 02 COLLECTION. *ABOVE:* EVERY LABEL CARRIES A NUMBER FROM 0 TO 23. A CIRCLE AROUND THE NUMBER IDENTIFIES THE COLLECTION FROM WHICH A GARMENT COMES. NUMBER '10' IS THE MENSWEAR COLLECTION, DESCRIBED AS 'A WARDROBE CONSISTING OF GARMENTS THAT HAVE DIFFERENT FUNCTIONS YET EACH OF WHICH SHOULD BE GIVEN A SIMILAR VALUE AND IMPORTANCE'. THIS IMAGE IS FROM PROMOTIONAL MATERIAL FOR THE AUTUMN/WINTER 03/04 COLLECTION.

Born in 1959, *MARGIELA* graduated in 1979 from the Royal Academy of Fine Arts in Antwerp, Belgium. He started out as assistant to Jean-Paul Gaultier and, in 1988, Margiela staged his own first show in Paris. In that same year he founded Maison Martin Margiela with Jenny Meirens. In 1996 and 1998, he was asked to participate at the Biennale of Contemporary Art exhibition in Florence, Italy, and in June 1997 an exhibition was dedicated to him and his work in the Museum Boijmans Van Beuningen in Rotterdam, The Netherlands. The exhibition then travelled to Kyoto and Tokyo in Japan, and New York.

Margiela is a highly conceptual fashion artist. In his collections themes such as the recycling of materials and the deconstruction of patterns and shapes are fused. He uses garments from markets and second-hand shops and new pieces, taking them apart and reassembling them to create unique items. His artisan approach focuses on the quality of materials in their purest form. The seams on his clothes often remain visible. He combines several materials, such as jute and plastic, with light and transparent fabrics, with details visible from the outside.

In 1994, his collection consisted of the best pieces from his previous collections. In 1997, he presented 'semi-couture': clothes that were only half finished and shown to the public on simple coat hangers. The instructions for use could be found on the film that accompanied the show.

As a comment against the fashion industry, Margiela often uses veiled models on the catwalk. His fashion presentations are challenging to his audience as they often take place in unorthodox locations including empty underground stations and playgrounds.

Hermès invited Margiela to design their women's collections in 1997. Although the choice of Margiela was surprising for the conservative couture house, it proved that it was possible to combine the traditional with the innovative. In 2000, Margiela opened his first shop in Tokyo. Shops in Osaka, Paris, Brussels and London followed, all communicating the distinct aesthetic that is clearly Margiela.

Margiela's clothes are sought after and wearable, despite his concept-driven collections and presentations. Basic garments, such as shirts, jeans and T-shirts, are reworked every season with minimal detail changes to progress their modernity. With a cult following of devotees especially fashion editors and the fashion press, Margiela has made an impact on contemporary menswear and will continue to influence generations of designers.

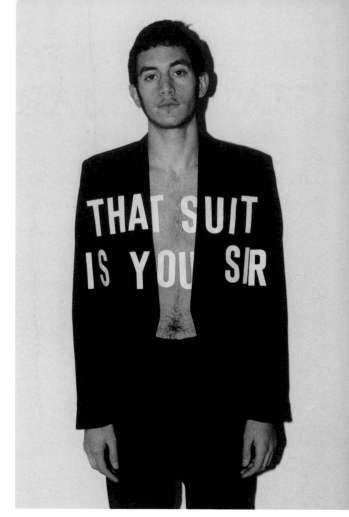

ABOVE: 'THAT SUIT IS YOU SIR' FROM THE SPRING/SUMMER 99 COLLECTION. *BELOW:* MARGIELA CONTINUALLY TRANSFORMS DENIM TO RETAIN ITS MODERNITY, AS IN THIS PIECE FOR SPRING/SUMMER 99. *OPPOSITE:* BLACK AND WHITE GARMENTS, AS SHOWN IN THIS OUTFIT FROM THE SPRING/SUMMER 02 COLLECTION, HAVE BECOME A SIGNATURE STYLE FROM MAISON MARTIN MARGIELA.

MAISON MARTIN MARGIELA

AN OUTFIT FROM SPRING/SUMMER 07.

1. *DESCRIBE YOUR MENSWEAR DESIGN PHILOSOPHY.*
   'Virility, individuality, masculinity without age.'

2. *WHAT IS THE MOST ENJOYABLE PART OF DESIGN?*
   'The conception, its research, the inspiration.'

3. *HOW WOULD YOU DESCRIBE YOUR CUSTOMER?*
   'Disparate, yet mainly from the creative fields.'

4. *HOW WOULD YOU DESCRIBE YOUR CREATIVE PROCESS AND WHAT FUELS YOUR DESIGN PROCESS?*
   'Continuous and drawn from day-to-day life with a reference to periods of our recent past where men
   were more resplendent than recently.'

5. *DOES YOUR DESIGN PROCESS ALWAYS FOLLOW THE SAME TRACK?*
   'Not always yet usually, like most things instinctive.'

6. *HOW WOULD YOU DEFINE SUCCESSFUL MENSWEAR?*
   'Invisible, melded with the person so much so that they both become one.'

7. *HOW IMPORTANT IS MASCULINITY IN MENSWEAR?*
   'Vital.'

8. *HOW WOULD YOU DESCRIBE CONTEMPORARY MENSWEAR?*
   'For the moment it seems to be eccentrically varied yet with a leaning towards 1980s music references.'

9. *HOW DO YOU KNOW WHEN A GARMENT IS 'COMPLETE'?*
   'You just do!'

10. *WHAT IS THE MOST CHALLENGING ASPECT OF DESIGN?*
    'Pushing forward yet remaining true to the authenticity of the garment.'

11. *HOW MANY OF YOUR MENSWEAR IDEAS ARE BASED ON TRADITION?*
    'Practically all, yet one man's tradition can be another's poison.'

12. *HOW ARE YOU PERSONALLY INNOVATIVE/MODERN WITH MENSWEAR?*
    'That's for others to decide we just "do", continue and hopefully grow.'

13. *HOW WOULD YOU DEFINE YOUR AESTHETIC?*
    'A sensibility, sensuality, a "self".'

MARC JACOBS

As an INTERNATIONAL FASHION ICON, Marc Jacobs has translated his APPRECIATION of worn-out, second-hand clothes into a global business. Constantly DRIVING FORWARD the fashion trend system, Jacobs has a significant influence on fashion. His menswear collections are defined by creating contemporary versions of RETRO CLASSICS. In celebrating the beauty of the ordinary, he ensures that his clothes always appear intrinsically of the moment.

While still at Parsons School of Art in New York, Jacobs, who was born in New York in 1963, designed his first hand-knitted sweater collection and sold it to Barbara Weiser at the well-known boutique Charivari. At college Jacobs won several awards, including the Perry Ellis Gold Thimble Award, before graduating in 1981. The following year, he was hired as womenswear designer at Perry Ellis and presented his first collection in 1986.

OPPOSITE, BACK: FOR AUTUMN/WINTER 07/08, MARC JACOBS DESIGNED A PREDOMINATELY GREY COLLECTION THAT CONFORMED TO THE BRAND'S DISTINCT WEARABILITY. **OPPOSITE, FRONT:** AS DESIGNER FOR LOUIS VUITTON, JACOBS ALSO CREATES LUXURIOUS CLOTHES FOR THE GLOBAL PARIS-BASED BRAND. MOD-STYLE TAILORING INSPIRED THE AUTUMN/WINTER 03/04 LINE. **RIGHT:** THE AUTUMN/WINTER 03/04 COLLECTION IS IN KEEPING WITH LOUIS VUITTON'S CLASSIC BUT CONTEMPORARY APPEAL.

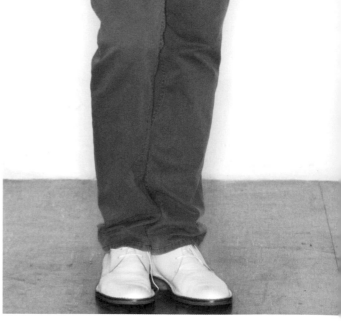

At Perry Ellis, *JACOBS* designed the infamous grunge collection in 1992. The concept was celebrated in fashion circles as revolutionary, but Jacobs was regarded as being too radical for Perry Ellis, and the American sportswear house ended his contract in 1992. Jacobs went on to win the Women's Designer of the Year Award from the CFDA (Council of Fashion Designers of America) in the same year, the youngest designer to receive the award.

Visually translating the clash and noise of the music of Pearl Jam and Nirvana into pattern and colour, Jacobs described the grunge collection as his best yet. One-dollar plaid shirts were sent to Italy and made into $1,000 silk shirts, while Birkenstock shoes were reproduced in satin. *'It was about a trodden down sort of glamour,'* explains Jacobs. *'I like the reverse snobbery of taking something that is mundane and everyday and making it deluxe.'* The American flag was transformed into cashmere blankets, as the grunge look became an influential trend across the globe.

In 1994, Jacobs, along with his business partner Robert Duffy, launched a womenswear collection and, in 1995, the first men's ready-to-wear collection debuted. It was based on pieces that Duffy and Jacobs wanted to have in their own wardrobes.

The first Marc Jacobs store opened in New York in 1997 and with it the first advertising campaign was launched. It featured Kim Gordon of Sonic Youth and was shot by Juergen Teller. The campaign began a collaboration that has gone on to feature a variety of contemporary directors, artists, models, musicians and actors. Like his clothes, Jacobs's campaigns always focus on the personality and credibility of the individuals involved.

Appointed creative director of Louis Vuitton in 1997, Jacobs created the company's first ready-to-wear collection. At Vuitton, Jacobs is credited with re-establishing the traditional accessory line as a contemporary fashion business. Jacobs collaborated with artists Steven Sprouse, to design the infamous graffiti bags for Spring 01, and Julie Verhoeven, who created patchwork collage bags, and with graphic artist Takashi Murakami, who contributed to the bubblegum-cute accessories for Spring/Summer 03. Jacobs's work for the French luxury house has established Louis Vuitton as the global leader in luxury goods. Because of their influence on the international catwalks, many of Jacobs's concepts created for Louis Vuitton have inspired high-street stores around the world.

ABOVE: UNPRETENTIOUS CASUAL GARMENTS ARE JACOBS'S SIGNATURE STYLE: THE PURPLE PANTS ARE FROM THE SPRING/ SUMMER 07 RANGE. *BELOW:* THE DIFFUSION LINE, MARC BY MARC JACOBS, HAS BEEN A HUGE COMMERCIAL SUCCESS, AND THE SPRING/SUMMER 07 COLLECTION WAS INSPIRED BY ARMY SURPLUS CLOTHING AND WAS SHOWN ON YOUTHFUL MODELS. *OPPOSITE:* AN EARLY MARC JACOBS COLLECTION FROM SPRING/ SUMMER 96 SHOWS THE DESIGNER'S APPRECIATION OF RELAXED UNCOMPLICATED CLOTHING.

REFOCUSING on his own name brand in 2001, Jacobs launched a diffusion line, Marc by Marc Jacobs, which has PROVED SO POPULAR that it is one of the first diffusion lines to threaten to OVERSHADOW THE MAIN COLLECTIONS.

MARC JACOBS

Jacobs's company now has a full range of products from perfume and eyewear to accessories and shoes, and he has opened stores all over the world. His success lies in his ability to design wearable and desirable clothes that appeal to a vast market. He believes that his customers are only interested in the final product and not the creative journey he followed to create it. *'People don't really care what a garment was inspired by. Nor do they care where a designer spends his holiday in order to come up with the idea. I think of fashion as more of a WHIM,'* explains Jacobs. *'Basically when we design we think about how can we take what we like from the past, update it and make it feel right for now.'* This retrospective concept is key to the success of Jacobs's clothes, which while still modern also have a subtle sense of nostalgia.

Despite Jacobs's fascination with the past he believes his clothes are still relevant to a contemporary market. *'I'm not trying to turn back the hands of time and say people should go back to the way they used to dress,'* he explains. *'What I do is retrospective in some ways but really it's contemporary as I make clothes that people want to wear today. I do have romantic ideas about the past, for example, I was only seven in the 1960s and remember thinking the clothes looked amazing.'*

It was during his studies at Parsons in New York in the late 1970s that Jacobs frequented the notorious dance clubs in the area, and he continues to use the spirit of that era as inspiration for his collections.

'It's about a CONSTANT RE-CELEBRATION of what turns us on,' he says. 'YOUTH, ENERGY, VITALITY, FREEDOM. Not in this pining for the past way, but again just constantly celebrating that its energy is STILL RELEVANT.'

Creating clothes that don't try too hard is exactly what Jacobs does best and this is the main reason why his clothes have such a global appeal. Jacobs himself does not want his clothes to communicate new philosophies or challenge perceptions on menswear. Instead, he believes that contemporary men want easy, conventional garments that do not suggest they are obsessed with fashion. He asserts that men want to be stylish rather than fashionable. As he says, *'I am a bit suspicious of men who follow fashion too closely.'*

ABOVE RIGHT: AN OUTFIT FROM THE SPRING/SUMMER 07 COLLECTION BY MARC JACOBS. CHOOSING TO SHOOT HIS GARMENTS ON 'CHARACTER MODELS', INSTEAD OF TRADITIONAL MODELS, HIGHLIGHTS JACOBS'S DESIRE TO CREATE STYLISH NOT FASHIONABLE CLOTHES. *OPPOSITE:* GARMENTS FROM THE MARC JACOBS AUTUMN/WINTER 06/07 COLLECTION. JACOBS'S CLOTHES ARE REMINISCENT OF THE PAST – USUALLY THE 1960s, 1970s AND 1980s – YET ALWAYS INCLUDE A CONTEMPORARY TAKE.

NE OF THE RARE PICTURES OF THE MYSTERY MAN OF MILLIONS

MEADHAM/KIRCHHOFF

Edward Meadham and Benjamin Kirchhoff are often informed by womenswear shapes, which they translate into menswear garments. PREDOMINANTLY MASCULINE, THEIR CLOTHES ARE INHERENTLY MODERN AND STYLISH. Their urban cool aesthetic balances diverse references and sources of inspiration that are rooted in the visual arts.

London-based design team Edward Meadham and Benjamin Kirchhoff launched their menswear label in 2002. French-born Kirchhoff and British Meadham met at Central St Martins College in London and soon after graduation launched their first collection. The team also designs womenswear, but it is the menswear line that established the brand. Their debut roused immediate interest from the press and Meadham/Kirchhoff has been integral to the recent resurgence of interest in contemporary British menswear.

OPPOSITE: A RESEARCH BOARD BY BENJAMIN KIRCHHOFF FOR THE AUTUMN/WINTER 07/08 COLLECTION ILLUSTRATES THE DIVERSE REFERENCES THAT INFORM THE DESIGN TEAM. *LEFT:* AN OUTFIT FROM THE SPRING/SUMMER 07 COLLECTION SHOWS MEADHAM/ KIRCHHOFF'S INNOVATIVE APPROACH TO FABRIC AND COLOUR.

Constantly described as Gothic designers, **_MEADHAM AND KIRCHHOFF_** have the ability to fuse diverse reference points, such as architecture and legends of the silver screen, to create wearable and masculine clothes. *'We are interested in the ideal of masculinity and redefining it as a concept,'* they explain. *'This is about considering what really is masculine, what are masculine proportions and how we can redefine the male body and not make it look awkward. We have never really been about boyishness but we've never been grown up either. We are very much about balance and we tend to go back to the same fabrics for a few seasons, and we have trademarks that we have used since the beginning.'* Creating a sensitive balance in their collections is what makes the garments wearable but still edgy and interesting.

Extensive research, according to Kirchhoff and Meadham, is key to their unique aesthetic, and it is always the most enjoyable part of the design process for them. The realization of the garment from drawing, observing and creating the details and fabric is the reward for months of initial research. Their inspiration is always diverse although it generally starts with films. *'In between collections we tend to watch a lot of movies of a specific genre and elements from them will influence us and inform the mood and style of the collection. For example, for SS06 we watched a lot of Cinecitta productions, for AW06/07 it was 1940s film noir and recently Cocteau and Genet films.'* Design icons include Jean Cocteau, Edward VIII when he was Prince of Wales and Jean-Paul Gaultier. *'For us it is trying to come up with something that is new and to communicate our ideas and concepts into a garment. We don't use a lot of clothing references when we design as we work with a mood so our message has to be understood somehow once the garment is realized.'*

The team describes a complete garment as when the balance of elements is right. They recognize that a lot of their menswear designs are derived from traditional techniques, not just tailoring but also the methodology of menswear. By this they mean that the placement of details and the right proportions are integral to successful menswear and they believe it is important to be extremely respectful of tradition. *'We are very much into the idea of Englishness in all its aspects: the eccentricity, the stiff upper lip, the humour, the ideal of liberty, the gloom and melancholia, the godlessness. It is not an easy concept to put together in words, but The Smiths express it very well, so do the films of Michael Powell and Emeric Pressburger, and the architecture of Nicholas Hawksmoor. I think we express an idealized interpretation of all these ideas. Also, as Benjamin grew up in Africa there is an element of that in the label, in the proportions of garments and in the use of cloth.'*

ABOVE: A RESEARCH COLLAGE BY BENJAMIN KIRCHHOFF FOR SPRING/SUMMER 07. THE PROPORTION OF COLOUR IN THE COLLECTION IS INTEGRAL TO ITS SUCCESS VERY EARLY ON IN THE DESIGN PROCESS. *OPPOSITE:* PROMOTIONAL IMAGES FOR THE SPRING/SUMMER 04 COLLECTION ILLUSTRATE MEADHAM/KIRCHHOFF'S EXPERIMENTAL APPROACH TO COMMUNICATING THEIR CLOTHES. CREATING A 'MOOD' FOR EACH SEASON IS KEY TO THE DESIGNERS.

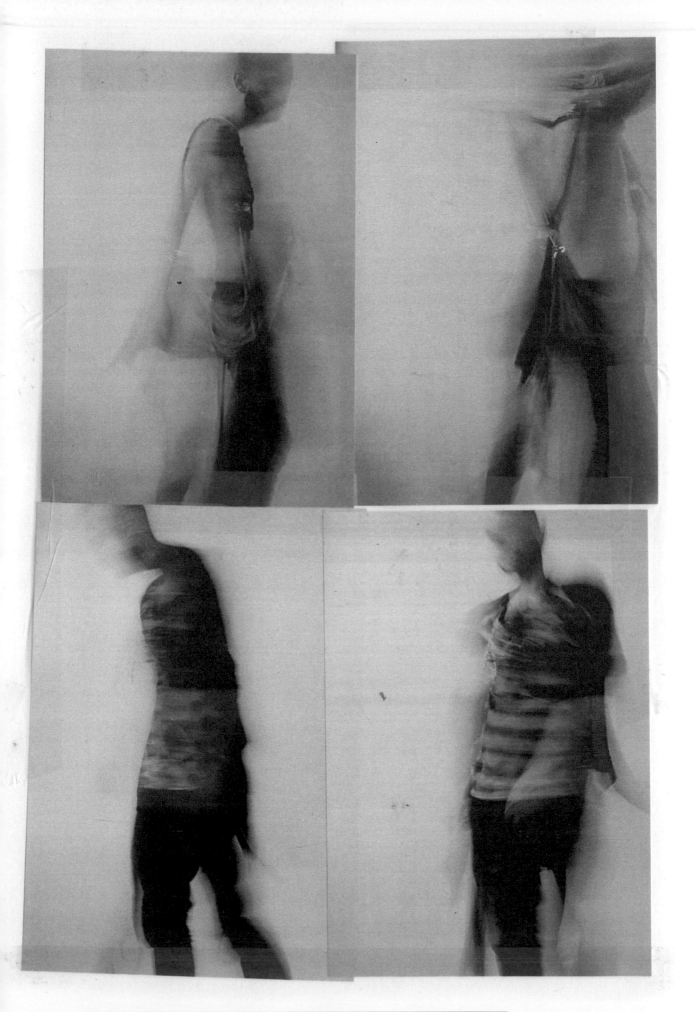

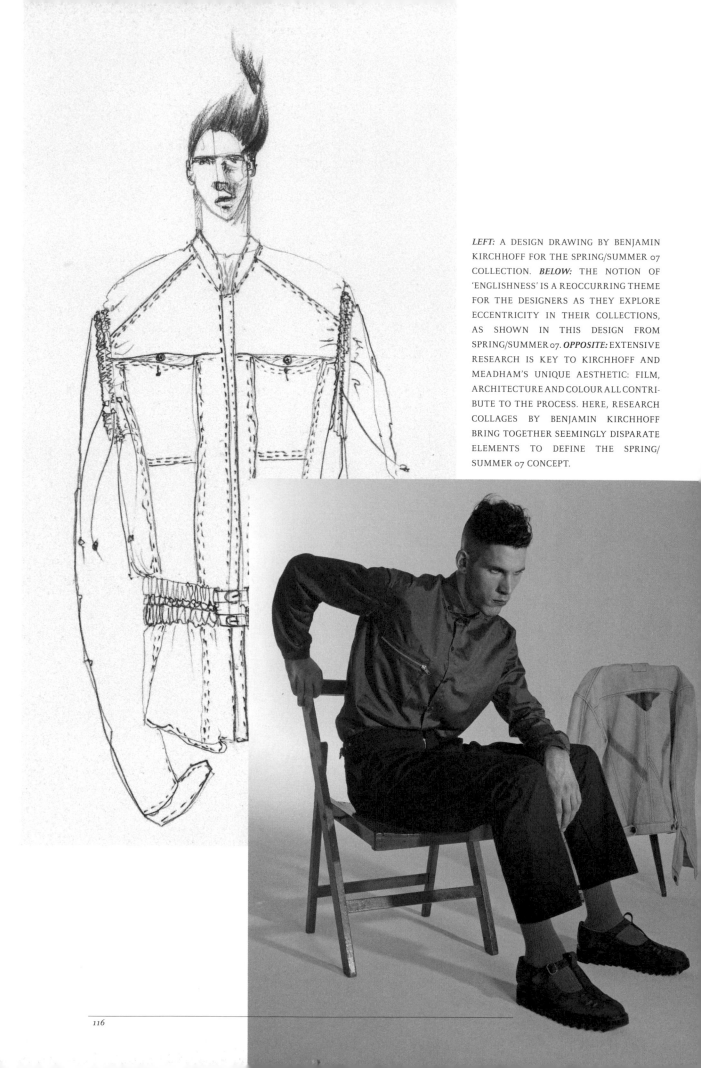

LEFT: A DESIGN DRAWING BY BENJAMIN KIRCHHOFF FOR THE SPRING/SUMMER 07 COLLECTION. *BELOW:* THE NOTION OF 'ENGLISHNESS' IS A REOCCURRING THEME FOR THE DESIGNERS AS THEY EXPLORE ECCENTRICITY IN THEIR COLLECTIONS, AS SHOWN IN THIS DESIGN FROM SPRING/SUMMER 07. *OPPOSITE:* EXTENSIVE RESEARCH IS KEY TO KIRCHHOFF AND MEADHAM'S UNIQUE AESTHETIC: FILM, ARCHITECTURE AND COLOUR ALL CONTRIBUTE TO THE PROCESS. HERE, RESEARCH COLLAGES BY BENJAMIN KIRCHHOFF BRING TOGETHER SEEMINGLY DISPARATE ELEMENTS TO DEFINE THE SPRING/ SUMMER 07 CONCEPT.

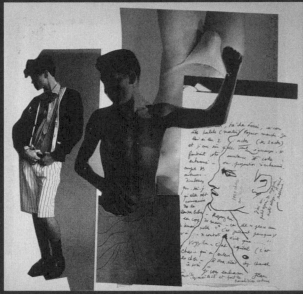

The team believes that the contemporary menswear market is buoyant. 'There are so many designers who design interesting clothing that is not gender specific, but for us MENSWEAR HAS TO REFLECT A SIDE OR SIDES OF MASCULINITY. MEN HAVE A DIFFERENT APPRECIATION OF CLOTHING, they have a much more fetishistic relationship to it and a successful label needs to appeal to that element.' Their customers, according to the team, are men with a strong and developed sense of style, WHO THINK INDEPENDENTLY OF TRENDS OR ESTABLISHED NOTIONS OF DRESS.

Kirchhoff and Meadham have an innovative and creative approach to design, and it is this sense of modernity that elevates their brand as a beacon for progressive British menswear. As well as creating six acclaimed menswear collections and running their label, the team has created footwear for high-street brand Topman. Working with shoe giant George Cox, pioneer of the 1950s 'brothel creeper' boot, they have mixed traditional styling details with their signature Gothic aesthetic.

Contemporary menswear, according to Kirchhoff and Meadham, is still developing, but more importantly there is now not just one style. There is a diverse range of exciting designers who are all projecting their very own design ideas and philosophies for dressing the contemporary man. *'Overall there is a sense that designers are trying to move forward many years of men's clothing,'* say Kirchhoff and Meadham, who are at the forefront of creating masculine-focused and directional clothing.

PATRIK SÖDERSTAM

The SWOOSH TROUSER and the SNAP SHIRT are just two examples of Söderstam's DYNAMIC CLOTHING CONCEPTS. Fusing sportswear, jeans and causal wear Söderstam creates garments that encourage a relationship with the people who want to wear them. The aesthetic is HYPER-BAGGY AND FANTASTICALLY CONTEMPORARY.

Patrik Söderstam describes himself as a clothes maker and 'multi talent'. He graduated from Central St Martins College in London in 2003, after studying at the Stockholm Cutting Academy in Sweden where he specialized in the construction of menswear. He has worked for British designer Robert Cary-Williams and also as a costume designer and stylist for Nokia, Nike and Absolut Vodka.

SHIRT
FABRIC—100% VISCOSE
COLOUR SILVER

PADDED SHOULDER
DETAIL

OPPOSITE: A BAGGY LIGHT DENIM JACKET FROM THE AUTUMN/ WINTER 05/06 'ROBIN' COLLECTION. BY USING INFORMAL FABRICS, SÖDERSTAM CREATES GARMENTS THAT APPEAR FAMILIAR BUT ARE INHERENTLY MODERN IN THEIR CONSTRUCTION. ***LEFT:*** A SKETCH FOR THE JACKET OPPOSITE.

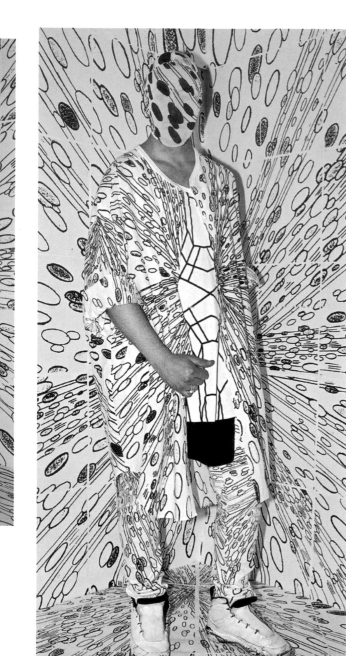

In asserting that his design aesthetic is driven by his own design ideals, **_PATRIK SÖDERSTAM_** says, '*I design with myself in mind. My design ideas circle around my life, what I need and how I want to express myself.*' He is interested in pushing boundaries and encouraging people to wear things that are out of the norm. '*I am not into theatrical things or expression; I am into real everyday life stuff. My style.*' Söderstam is not concerned with running a commercially driven business, making money or pleasing the customer. Rather, his need is to express himself in a progressive way that is achieved through his clothing and also through photography, graphics, sculptures and other artforms. '*I want to be involved in things that explore and open up the human mind and consciousness,*' he explains. '*Things that tickle my own and other people's brains and that look at how we see and think about ourselves, the everyday life we are living and what we do with it.*'

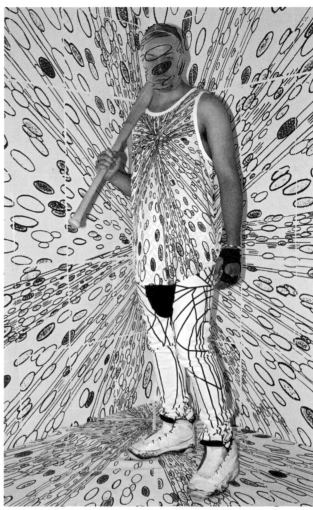

He believes his designs always attempt to *RELATE TO THE CULTURE* that is around or has been around. '*I try and take it to another level or ANOTHER DIMENSION. My clothes are MORPHED INTO OTHER SHAPES in this other world and then let loose onto the streets again. My aesthetic recipe is the play with EXTREME PROPORTIONS, FUTURISTIC DETAILING, TRASH and SEX, and a whole lot of OTHERNESS.*'

TIGHT PANTS CONTRASTING WITH OVERSIZED TOPS, OR VICE VERSA, ARE FUNDAMENTAL TO SÖDERSTAM'S CONTEMPORARY SILHOUETTE. THE 'DOT EXPLOSION' BACKGROUND SIMULATES THE PATTERN ON THE GARMENTS FROM HIS ENERGETIC 'ORGASM' COLLECTION IN 2003. *OVERLEAF:* THE 'TV' COLLECTION FROM AUTUMN/WINTER 04/05 SAW SÖDERSTAM EXPERIMENT WITH TOP-HEAVY SHAPES. THE BUILT-UP CALF AREA ON THE TROUSERS HAS BECOME A SIGNATURE STYLE.

Avant-garde shapes are key to Söderstam's distinct style. His silhouette usually consists of skinny jeans, renowned for having built-up and padded calves, and voluminous over-sized tops. 'For me, volume is the big thing. I always want it really big,' he explains. 'There is so much detailing in menswear that you can play with, so many roles and codes to break down and do something new with. Other things like prints and fabrics have also not been investigated thoroughly yet. There are a lot of things you can be inspired by from womenswear, but again the trick is to balance it with masculinity.'

Masculinity is still important to Söderstam's clothes. 'As I go to the extreme a lot of the time, it is important for me to always try not to go too far and make clothes for a clown. I want to feel comfortable, secure and masculine. I want people, the other sex in my case, to see me as a masculine man. A bit of a different man, though.'

According to Söderstam, the design process is intimate and enjoyable. He works in his design studio by himself and enjoys experimenting with new shapes. 'I like the process of making new patterns to make up test garment after test garment.' His project is eternal. 'I am working on the same project all the time. This is a collection of garments I need for my life. I would like to get it done so I can go on with other projects, maybe for someone other than myself. I am not very happy with what I have come up with yet so I will continue experimenting until I have a wardrobe that I feel I can live in. I am constantly working on a couple of different garments that I want to do better. They evolve and come out in different shapes, cuts and colours.'

Söderstam has limited ambitions to be commercially successful. 'Up to now my design process always follows the same track. There are enough people who design for the trendy masses and change from season to season. I would like to think of my work as more primal and conceptual; something I need to do for myself. To sell clothes and make money out of it is not what I have in mind at all at this point.'

Despite Söderstam's aim to work for only himself, he does relish the challenge of presenting his garments in a creative context. He communicates his concepts through photographs, graphics and film.

'I don't like doing the traditional catwalk with models. I hate that. I will probably need to do catwalks again at some point, but it is all so boring. I AM INTO PROGRESSIVE PRESENTATIONS. I think women look great on the catwalk as I look at them and see them as beautiful sexy sculptures, but men just don't work up there for me.'

Söderstam does accept that there are others who want to wear his visionary garments, and he likes to think of his customers as open-minded thinkers. 'They are arty rebels that know what they are about. They are not slaves to the trends that are around.'

Unlike many of his contemporaries, Söderstam is happy to move away from the associations of traditional menswear. 'I try to work against tradition. I don't like the word. I grew up in a small village where tradition was a religion and I always wanted to break away from that.'

To be modern in design is very important to Söderstam, and he takes on this challenge every day. His aim is to design something that no one has done before. 'Contemporary menswear is about finding new ways of dressing for a man. Clothes that go away from the traditional and conservative ways of dressing but keep the masculinity progressive and experimental.'

His radical menswear collections have made an impact in the cities in which they have been promoted, including London, Stockholm, Tokyo, Paris and New York. With titles as challenging as the clothes, the collections have been called 'I Woke Up', 'The Sid', 'TV', 'Orgasm', 'Oof!', 'Puking Beauty', 'Stretch', 'Reversible', 'Burberry War' and 'Black Denim'. Successful menswear for Söderstam is something that allows a man to express himself in the same way as a woman, but in a masculine fashion, 'something that shows your own personality and not just an attitude.'

PAUL SMITH

Famed for his international commercial success, Paul Smith HAS SOLD BRITISHNESS GLOBALLY. Translating his FERVENT INTEREST in collecting into collections, Smith has the ability to communicate and CELEBRATE DIVERSE INSPIRATIONS. His idiosyncratic take on traditional British classic designs with a twist has enabled his menswear to retain its MODERNITY AND ACCESSIBILITY.

'I design clothes that are for the wearer to enjoy,' explains Smith, who has become a beacon for British fashion and style. 'This means simple classical shapes often with secrets such as a different colour for one button, unusual buttons, interesting lining fabrics.' The Paul Smith brand, which has developed into a global business empire, originated from a clear aesthetic, which Smith describes as, 'A curious mind mixing the past and the present, the kitsch and the beautiful, but always with a sense of humour.'

<u>*PAUL SMITH'S*</u> initiation into fashion was unique. With dreams of becoming a professional cyclist, he had a terrible accident that ruled out this career path. At the age of 17, with no certain plans, he met a group of inspirational art students who introduced him to an exciting world of creativity and new ideas.

Inspired by the world of design, Smith opened his first shop in Nottingham, England in 1970 and, using a small amount of savings, he enrolled in evening classes to study tailoring. By 1976, Smith had shown his first menswear collection in Paris under the Paul Smith brand.

Within 20 years, Smith had established himself as a successful British designer, combining in his clothes a sense of humour with an appreciation of tradition and the classics. *'I suppose that a lot of my work is based on tradition,'* he comments, *'reusing traditional fabrics in a new way or traditional methods of manufacturing, but always giving them a new twist.'*

Renowned for his design process, he states that he never actually draws. Instead, he fills notebooks with ideas and inspirational material. *'I never sit down consciously and design. For me, ideas flow all the time and I have notebooks full of thoughts. I think my main ability is observation and through this I get my ideas. Normally I accumulate my ideas for each of the many lines that I design and then I present them to each design team. They then progress the ideas and turn them into reality, but with regular meetings with me. The process more or less stays the same.'*

By constantly fine-tuning his design eye, Smith is well aware of his customers' requirements. He describes his customer as *'someone who enjoys clothes and wants to look good but not stand out as being someone who seeks attention. Often my customers are creative people who are quite confident in themselves.'*

A designer's approach to masculinity is one way in which Smith believes designers can define themselves. *'It depends on the designer and the audience of the designer. In my case, I think generally speaking there is masculinity in my work, even though sometimes the shirts could be floral or the jacket could be embroidered. Essentially I design clothes that are popular but still have something special.'*

PAGES 124–125: ALTHOUGH CRAFTSMANSHIP, CLASSICISM AND TRADITION ARE KEY TO PAUL SMITH'S COLLECTIONS, HE IS ABLE TO CREATE CONTEMPORARY CLOTHES. FOR SPRING/SUMMER 07 HE USED LIGHTWEIGHT FABRICS IN MODERN SHAPES. *OPPOSITE:* CASUAL TAILORING IS FUNDAMENTAL TO PAUL SMITH'S COLLECTIONS; THESE OUTFITS FROM SPRING/SUMMER 07 ALSO SHOW HIS SENSITIVE APPROACH TO COLOUR. *BACKGROUND IMAGE:* PAUL SMITH IS AN AVID COLLECTOR OF THE DECORATIVE ARTS, SO MUCH SO THAT HE OPENED A CURIOSITY SHOP IN LONDON'S MAYFAIR TO SHOWCASE HIS ECLECTIC PIECES.

Modern menswear, according to Smith, is concerned with FUSING CRAFTSMANSHIP WITH MODERNITY. 'To be contemporary, clothes must have elements of CRAFTSMANSHIP, CLASSICISM and TRADITION, but always WITH A MODERN ASPECT such as a modern fabric or cut/shape.' Knowing when to stop the design process is also an important part of Smith's work. 'It's a skill that you learn through experience; IT JUST FEELS RIGHT at some point.'

The Paul Smith business has grown to encompass twelve collections, which include womenswear, childrenswear, watches, furniture, rugs, china, spectacles and fragrances. Designed both in Nottingham and London, the collections are primarily produced in England and Italy, while the fabrics used are from Italy, France and Britain.

In 2002, Smith collaborated with Cappellini to create a collection of furniture called Mondo, which was influenced by his observations and travel. In 2003, he designed an upholstery textile in partnership with textile company Maharam. It was called Bespoke and was inspired by classic pinstripe suiting. *'Most of my design icons are architects or product designers,'* says Smith. He cites such people as *'Toyo Ito, an architect whose work is creative, organic but usable, or some of the Italian design heroes like Joe Colombo or Vico Magistretti.'*

The Paul Smith name has become truly global. The collection is sold in more than 35 countries, and Smith owns 24 shops and has 38 franchises worldwide, as well as over 200 shops in Japan. Shops are also found in London, Nottingham, Paris, Milan, New York, Hong Kong, Singapore, Taiwan, the Philippines, Korea, Kuwait and China.

As designer and chairman, Smith continues to be an integral part of the company. Consequently, he remains fully involved in every aspect of the business and says that his success is down to *'lateral thinking and by not going down the obvious route, and by mixing things in a way that is not expected.'*

Smith's contribution to modern menswear lies in his creative sensibility and his ability to fuse commercial products with a distinct reflection on British quirkiness. While his clothes are always wearable, they also communicate a modernity that portrays the current mood within menswear design.

OPPOSITE: RED EAR, THE LIMITED-EDITION CLOTHING LINE BY PAUL SMITH, INTRODUCED PATCHWORK DENIM JEANS IN SPRING/ SUMMER 04. *RIGHT:* INSPIRATION BOARDS BY THE PAUL SMITH DESIGN TEAM ILLUSTRATE HOW MANY INFLUENCES ARE BROUGHT TOGETHER IN A COLLECTION.

PAUL SMITH

PETER JENSEN

Danishman Peter Jensen has acquired the knack of presenting SELF-DEPRECATING SHOWS. His charming visions have gently influenced the international fashion scene by promoting his distinctive Scandinavian sensibility. Often 'NERDY', Jensen's menswear clothes are defined by their QUIRKY DETAILS AND AN IRONIC TAKE ON CLASSIC GARMENTS.

Known for designing light-hearted menswear collections, Peter Jensen has the unique ability to unite wit with wearable clothes. Jensen has positioned himself as an innovator who is committed to creating individual, subtle and well-crafted clothing.

OPPOSITE: FOR HIS SPRING/SUMMER 05 SHOW, PETER JENSEN PRESENTED HIS COLLECTION ON AN ICE RINK. THE MODELS' FACES WERE PAINTED BLACK, AND THE NUMBERS INDICATED THE ORDER OF THE SKATERS. PHOTOGRAPHY BY MAURO COCILIO. *RIGHT:* THIS IMAGE IS BY ÅBÄKE, THE GRAPHIC DESIGN GROUP WHO COLLABORATED WITH PETER JENSEN ON HIS AUTUMN/WINTER 02/03 COLLECTION. THE LINING OF THE JACKET IS A PATCHWORK OF OLD T-SHIRTS.

Prior to his arrival in the UK, _**JENSEN**_ undertook a rigorous education in his native Denmark. He started making clothes at an evening class on sewing when he was 12. _'I grew up in a home where there was a sewing machine and a lot of knitting. To me, those kinds of handcrafts felt very secure. It was a cosy environment, with your mum and your gran sitting there knitting and talking. I enjoyed being with them more than with my dad, for instance, who would be outdoors doing things that didn't feel so secure. I liked being at the sewing machine and doing things alone.'_

Born and bred in Løgstør, Denmark, Jensen studied embroidery for six months, graphic design for a year and tailoring for two years before he finally took a BA in fashion design at the Denmark Design School in Copenhagen. Moving to London in 1997, Jensen studied for a Masters degree at Central St Martins College, where he graduated with distinction in 1999.

Immediately after graduation, Jensen launched his distinctive menswear collection, which was sold through London boutique The Library. His third menswear collection was shown on the official schedule of the Chambre Syndicale du Prêt-à-Porter in Paris.

Inspiration for the collections comes from a wide variety of sources, including his home country of Denmark. There is never a specific or obvious theme, as an important aspect of each collection is that each garment should work by itself. _'They are designed as "pieces" that don't necessarily go together,'_ explains Jensen. _'We don't work on silhouettes. Many of the reference points are really ordinary: a shirt, for instance. From there, we work on the details and the atmosphere. We design flat, from pattern, not on a mannequin. In that sense, you are steadily creating a language of clothes rather than a biannual fashion spectacle.'_

Each season Jensen is inspired by a different female personality, who becomes a muse for his womenswear collection, and this in turn informs his menswear. _'We don't pick a different muse for the menswear: the same theme runs through both. We always show our menswear as part of our womenswear presentation. The personality acts as the stimulus for a collection more than dictating its literal appearance.'_

Jensen is also praised for his witty and innovative fashion presentations. For Spring/Summer 05, he used an ice rink for a spectacular fashion show on ice. Entitled 'Tonya', the show was a tribute to the disgraced ice skater Tonya Harding. Jensen's other shows have included 'Gertrude' (Stein), 'Alison' (Steadman, the actress) and 'Nancy' (Mitford). Despite the female muse, the men's collection is made first. It begins with research, which blends into the design process. As Jensen was trained in menswear, he views this as a natural starting point.

LEFT: JENSEN HAS A COMMERCIAL APPROACH TO HIS DESIGN, AS HE WANTS HIS CLOTHES TO BE SOLD AND TO BE WORN. THIS OUTFIT, FROM THE AUTUMN/WINTER 05/06 COLLECTION, SHOWS JENSEN'S ABILITY TO PRODUCE REFINED CLOTHES THAT AVOID ANY UNNECESSARY DETAILS. *ABOVE:* THE SPRING/SUMMER 07 COLLECTION WAS NAMED 'TINA' AFTER TINA BARNEY, THE AMERICAN ART PHOTOGRAPHER.

PETER JENSEN

'You are working within a set of rules in menswear. I'M DEFINITELY NOT A GREAT FAN OF THE WEIRD. There is something nice about a good suit, for instance. If you can work within those rules, that's the mark of whether you're any good or not.'

Design partner Gerard Wilson works on all the collections too, and between them they make important decisions on the wearability of the collections. *'The consistency in menswear is probably more a reflection of Gerard's and my opinions about clothes,'* affirms Jensen. *'Because we are men, it's more natural to work out who would wear those clothes. It's more difficult to know what you would wear if you were a woman. With menswear, it's instinctive.'*

A feminine touch has become a signature of Jensen's menswear. The garments often have an element of the handcrafted about them – appliqué, embroidery or sewing – which has become a strong part of the Jensen 'handwriting'. *'It's only Gerard, me and about five interns in the studio,'* explains Jensen. *'It's a real struggle, therefore, maintaining that level of quality in your work, whilst realizing that there are only a limited number of people that want to pay for it. Often, you end up sitting there, hand-sewing everything!'*

Although Jensen's design process has been much documented and communicated, it is the product that Jensen believes is most important. He firmly asserts that his audience and customers have no real interest in his design journey. Jensen wants his clothes to be sold and, of course, to be worn. This commercial approach, which inherently retains Jensen's quirky and humorous identity, has translated internationally, with Japan being a strong market. Jensen thinks that this is due to an appreciation of his approach to print and colour, which is integral to each collection. *'There is such an emphasis on novelty there; we are under a lot of pressure to renew ourselves constantly.'*

Jensen has built up strong relationships within the fashion industry and has been consistently supported through ongoing developments with Topshop. Autumn/Winter 06/07 saw the launch of an affordable, but characteristically Jensen, line for high-street store Topman. Jensen also continues to work with cult shoe brand Buddahood, collaborating on a successful footwear line.

As head of menswear at Central St Martins College, Jensen finds he is fascinated by other design processes. *'You see these people with all the time in the world to work on a project because they don't have any production or business pressures. You advise them, help them source fabrics. I'm quite good at spotting what's gone wrong with their direction by looking at the details. When teaching, I try hard to distance myself from my own approach. You have to guide people regardless of their taste.'*

Peter Jensen successfully and wittily uses his Danish sensibility to produce charming contemporary clothes and to propel menswear design forward.

OPPOSITE: THE SPRING/SUMMER 06 COLLECTION WAS CALLED 'SISSY' AFTER SISSY SPACEK. THE GARMENTS EXUDE CHARM AND AN UNDERSTATED INNOCENCE. *ABOVE:* FOR HIS AUTUMN/WINTER 04/05 COLLECTION, JENSEN WAS INSPIRED BY HANDS AND MANY OF THE MOTIFS IN THE PRINTS AND PATTERNS WERE DRAWN FROM THE COVERS OF OLD AGATHA CHRISTIE PAPERBACKS.

Conversation with Peter Jensen courtesy of Penny Martin.

RAF SIMONS

Raf Simons is one of the key innovators in contemporary menswear. His collections are defined by a NARROW, LINEAR CUT and are often shown on teenagers, rather than professional models. The clothes combine SARTORIAL TRADITIONS with the 'uniforms' of REBELLIOUS YOUTH. His groundbreaking work has signalled a MAJOR TURNING POINT IN THE REDEFINITION OF MEN'S CLOTHING.

Born in 1968 in Belgium, Raf Simons studied industrial design at the Antwerp Royal Academy. During his time at college he undertook an internship in Paris with Walter Van Beirendonck, who was part of the Antwerp Six group of designers. It is here that he became interested in the work of contemporary designers such as Martin Margiela and Jean-Paul Gaultier. Graduating in 1991, he worked for several years as a furniture designer for galleries and interiors.

OPPOSITE: RAF SIMONS MARKED TEN YEARS IN THE FASHION INDUSTRY WITH AN ELABORATE SHOW IN FLORENCE'S BOBOLI GARDENS SHOWING HIS SPRING/SUMMER 06 COLLECTION. *THIS PAGE:* THE SPRING/SUMMER 02 COLLECTION WAS INSPIRED BY MIDDLE EASTERN DRESS. COVERED HEADS AND FACES HIDDEN BEHIND SCARVES CAUSED CONTROVERSY AS SIMONS WAS CRITICIZED FOR PROMOTING 'TERRORIST CHIC'. *OVERLEAF:* INSPIRED BY MUSIC STYLE ICONS KRAFTWERK, SIMONS USED A STRICT COLOUR PALETTE OF BLACK, WHITE AND SHADES OF PALE GREY IN HIS SPRING/SUMMER 05 COLLECTION. THE INDUSTRIAL AND MODERN ENVIRONMENT ECHOED THE CLEAN SHARP LINES OF THE CLOTHES.

In a radical change of profession, supported by Linda Loppa, who was head of fashion at the Antwerp Royal Academy, **_RAF SIMONS_** went to work for a Belgian tailor before launching his first collection in 1995.

In 1999, he successfully designed two seasons for the menswear collection of Ruffo Research, a project by the Tuscan fashion company Ruffo aimed at collaborating with young designers to create contemporary fashion collections. In a dramatic decision, Simons shut down his company in 2000 to *'re-energize his reason to work and to take time to consider new directions'*. In the same year, Simons was appointed head professor of fashion at the University of Applied Arts in Vienna, Austria. The following year he reopened the label with a smaller team of collaborators. In 2005, he became creative director for the Jil Sander label, owned by the Prada Group. He also announced the creation of his second own menswear line, 'Raf by Raf Simons', which was launched in 2006.

During the mid-1990s, Simons was part of the influential wave of avant-garde Belgian designers that made an impact on the international fashion circuit. When Simons launched his first menswear collection he explained his design philosophy, *'I don't want to show clothes, I want to show my attitude, my past, present and future. I use memories and future visions and try to place them in today's world.'* His clothes are concerned with communicating the fact that he is inspired by the *'pride in individuality'*. Youth culture and its associations heavily inform his collections as he designs for what he describes as *'confident outsiders'*. His references to youth movements such as punk, goth and mod are not meant to be retrospective; rather, Simons translates their original energy into contemporary visions of confidence and modernity.

Simons's clothes are renowned for their IMPECCABLE CUT and CONTEMPORARY DESIGN AESTHETIC. However, he widely acknowledges that clothes are not his main focus. He cites MUSIC, ART, PERFORMANCE, IMAGES and WORDS as the inspiration behind his garments.

His book, *Raf Simons Redux*, defines his menswear vision. Published in 2005 to celebrate his ten-year anniversary, the book examines the modern male's psyche. It also illustrates Simons's design process and the inspiration he takes from the rebellion of past and present youth cultures, blending them with tradition to create modern alternatives for dressing.

Following his Spring/Summer 00 collection, Simons published another book, entitled *Isolated Heroes*, which consisted of images created in collaboration with photographer David Sims. Simons shared Sims's vision of not using traditional models, instead favouring individuals who were not noticed by the world but presented an alternative individual beauty.

For the February 2001 issue of British style magazine *i-D*, Simons was invited to be a special guest editor. With Francesco Bonami from the Museum of Contemporary Art Chicago, Simons curated the exhibition 'The Fourth Sex' at Pitti Immagine trade show in Florence in 2003. He also curated the exhibition 'Guides by Heroes' at the Municipal Fashion Museum in Hasselt, Belgium in the same year.

Simons's fashion shows are integral to communicating his radical concepts. He chooses locations that are not well known to a fashion audience. These have included industrial garages, rooftops and grand gardens. Working against the prescribed images of masculinity and identity seen in fashion magazines and advertising imagery, Simons only uses non-professional models who are often scouted on the streets of Paris and Antwerp.

By promoting the use of real people as models, Simons is not only avoiding the trappings of the fashion system, he is also focusing on designing clothes for real people that will actually be worn. He develops relationships with his 'models' and responds to their critiques of his collections. Simons concentrates on developing a language of communication with a specific generation, so the wearers' opinions and participation are vital in the design process. He says that he is always more interested in the language and meaning that is communicated when designing clothes than in just creating clothes that sell.

His design aesthetic has proven highly influential globally. He has been described as one of the most important innovators of menswear by the international press, '*Even now, 10 years on, there is a sense of something hatching – latent sexuality and incipient manhood – in the powerful collections that have made Simons, 37, a menswear star,*' explained Suzy Menkes in the *International Herald Tribune* in 2005. His clothes are available in shops around Europe, Japan, Hong Kong, Taiwan, the United States and Russia.

The menswear garments that Simons designs always present a modern and progressive silhouette. He likes to use techno fabrics, such as neoprene, which are layered and cut into contemporary shapes. Innovative techniques, such as laser cutting, are employed to create avant-garde pieces. His often industrial and dark style fuses strongly cut classic menswear with baggy street-wear influences. Simons may appear to design clothes that are preoccupied with adolescence and the aggression that is associated with the sub-cultures, but what he really masters is the presentation of radical visions that push menswear forward. His clothes may be challenging to some, but with youth culture as his driving force they are always inspiring and directional.

OPPOSITE: A DIFFUSION LINE, RAF BY RAF SIMONS, WAS LAUNCHED IN SPRING/SUMMER 06 AND CONSISTED OF PIECES SUCH AS HOODED TOPS IN STRONG COLOURS, ELONGATED TANK TOPS AND JEANS. SHOWN HERE IS A BLACK HOODIE FROM THE SPRING/SUMMER 07 COLLECTION. *ABOVE:* STRIPED JEANS FROM RAF BY RAF SIMONS'S AUTUMN/WINTER 07/08 COLLECTION.

RICK OWENS

A dynamic, sometimes washed-out aesthetic combining BOTH GRUNGE AND GLAMOUR is key to Rick Owens's men's collections. JUXTAPOSING MILITARY AND SPORTS INFLUENCES, Owens's rock styling ensures a contemporary edge for his garments. Reacting against the consumerism of his native Los Angeles, Owens often CELEBRATES THE ANTI-HERO.

Described as an 'indie' designer and known as a rock star favourite in Los Angeles, Rick Owens certainly produces clothes that are distinct. Born in California in 1961, Owens studied art at Parsons School of Design in New York before opting to take a two-year course in pattern making. He worked as a pattern cutter for several sportswear companies, before deciding to launch his own label in 1994. He sold his clothes through small boutiques and gradually built up an impressive client list including Madonna and Courtney Love. His reputation grew quickly and this led him to the attention of a group of Italian manufacturers, with whom he is now in partnership. In 2002, Owens won the Council of Fashion Designers of America (CFDA) Perry Ellis Award for Emerging Talent, and the following year he moved to Paris, where he presents his men's catwalk collection twice a year.

OPPOSITE, BACKGROUND: RICK OWENS BELIEVES THAT HIS CUSTOMERS RESPOND TO THE ATMOSPHERE OF HIS CLOTHES, AND HE COMMUNICATES THIS IN DARK AND MOROSE PRESENTATIONS. THE IMAGE SHOWN HERE IS TAKEN FROM THE AUTUMN/WINTER 06/07 COLLECTION. **OPPOSITE, FRONT:** COMBINING BOTH AN URBAN GLAMOUR AND GRUNGE IN HIS COLLECTIONS, OWENS ENSURES THAT HIS CLOTHES ARE ALWAYS FUNCTIONAL AND WEARABLE. THESE IMAGES ARE OF THE 'DRAKE' COLLECTION FOR SPRING/ SUMMER 07. **ABOVE:** LONG HAIR AND WAFER-THIN MODELS DEFINE OWENS'S ROCK STAR AESTHETIC, AS SHOWN IN THIS IMAGE FROM THE AUTUMN/WINTER 06/07 COLLECTION.

A minimalist palette combined with dramatic structure defines **OWENS'S** work, which is often described as being purely Gothic. Owens describes his designs as subtle and not sensational. Usually dark toned, draped and deconstructed, his designs reference glamour, with a glam-rock edge and broken-down ease that appears to be the very opposite to his Hollywood roots. *'I like severity and uniforms,'* he explains. *'I read somewhere once that Jean-Michel Frank, the furniture and interiors designer from the 1930s, had 40 identical grey flannel double-breasted suits in his closet. That combination of restraint and extravagance always stuck with me.'*

Characterized by fitted jackets and soft slouchy knits, Owens's menswear frames the body. He successfully manages to combine both glamour and grunge in his outfits. His work is never conceptual as his clothes are always functional. *'Where women have leeway to express their sensuality or even coquettishness, I sense that men are more attracted to projecting dignity and gravitas. I try to fill that order.'*

Masculinity is paramount to Owens. However, without a moment of mad flamboyance, *'it would be dull as dirt,'* he says. *'With both men and women, I'm kind of more into how a garment feels than how it looks. Personal luxury and a discreet tone is what I'm going after more than display or status.'*

For Owens, the design process is continuous. He carries around with him index cards in his back pocket and continually writes down notes and draws rough sketches. *'Especially at the gym or on a plane. When it's time to start a collection, I accumulate all the cards, edit them, and see what comes out.'* One of Owens's bibles is Paul Virilio's *Bunker Archaeology*, a book documenting the concrete bunkers built on the Atlantic coast in France during the occupation by the Germans. *'The simple alien shapes and their repetitive ominous style continually inspire me. In the pictures, they're empty, abandoned and slightly poignant. I hypnotize myself into my favourite space when I look through them.'*

Helmut Berger and Neil Young are also inspirations for Owens. Film director Visconti has Berger endlessly riding a golden sleigh through the snow to Wagner's music in *Ludwig*. *'Those cheekbones and sharp-shouldered uniforms and plumed helmets are unforgettable. Add his slightly euro-wicked reputation in the 1970s when I was growing up and he's kind of irresistible. Neil Young has a dignified integrity smudged with the hint of past mistakes that I think any man would like to identify with.'*

Recognizing his own pleasure in creating a garment that feels right when it is finished, Owens says, *'The most enjoyable part of design is sliding into something and realizing it came out just right. A garment is complete when you don't think you'll feel like a dick walking out the door in it.'* He relishes providing people with clothes they enjoy wearing. His clients, he believes, respond to the atmosphere of his clothes. *'My customer is probably someone who's been through a very flamboyant phase and is now playing with a severe anonymity.'*

Traditional menswear is a key reference in Owens's work. *'Pretty much all of my menswear is based on tradition. I know that when I see someone mix traditional codes successfully, it projects intelligence and attractively loose boundaries to me.'* Owens modernizes his take on traditional tailoring by exaggerating the proportions of his garments and ensuring that the fabrics feel broken down and worn in.

In 2006, Owens caused controversy in Florence with an installation featuring a realistic wax sculpture of himself urinating. The exhibition also showcased his furniture and a career retrospective that illustrated his dark aesthetic.

Based in Paris, Owens designs collections for both men and women, a fur line named Palais Royal, after the address of his Paris flagship store, and a furniture line.

PAGES 144–45: THE 'DUSULATOR' COLLECTION FOR AUTUMN/WINTER 06/07 WAS PRESENTED AT PITTI UOMO, THE FLORENCE TRADE SHOW. OWENS JUXTAPOSED MILITARY AND SPORTS INFLUENCES AND PORTRAYED A POST-APOCALYPTIC ENVIRONMENT THROUGH THE USE OF A DARK COLOUR PALETTE. *ABOVE, INTERIOR PHOTOGRAPHS:* THE RICK OWENS STORE IN PARIS MIRRORS THE SHARP DESIGN DIRECTION OF HIS COLLECTIONS: MODERN AND MONOCHROME. *ABOVE, FAR RIGHT:* A MODEL MARCHES THE RUNWAY FOR THE AUTUMN/WINTER 06/07 COLLECTION. *OPPOSITE:* FOR OWENS, THE DESIGN PROCESS CONSTANTLY EVOLVES. HE ALWAYS CARRIES INDEX CARDS WITH HIM AND OFTEN JOTS DOWN NOTES AND DRAWS ROUGH SKETCHES: 'WHEN IT'S TIME TO START A COLLECTION, I ACCUMULATE ALL THE CARDS, EDIT THEM AND SEE WHAT COMES OUT,' HE EXPLAINS.

Owens's philosophy when designing menswear is to give his customers a *VEHICLE FOR EXPRESSION OR NON-EXPRESSION*, as he describes it, *'NOT CARING WHO YOU IMPRESS IS ONE OF THE BIGGEST LUXURIES OF ALL'.*

SIV STØLDAL

Through her work, Norwegian Siv Støldal focuses on a garment's history and ASPIRES TO UNDERSTAND WHAT CLOTHES MEAN TO THE INDIVIDUAL. As a powerful method of communication, each collection, carefully guided by Støldal, explores some of the unknown territory of menswear design. Her clothes have a DISTINCT FORTUITOUS QUALITY.

Born in Norway in 1973, Siv Støldal now works and lives in London. Following three years' training in menswear tailoring in Bergen, Norway, Støldal went on to graduate from Central St Martins College in London in 1999. She launched her first collection, entitled 'Bob James', in 2000. She has exhibited her work in Norway, Paris and London and attracts international recognition.

OPPOSITE: STØLDAL'S RESEARCH FOR THE SCARECROW COLLECTION IN AUTUMN/WINTER 01/02 INVOLVED ASKING 7 PEOPLE IN 7 HOUSES ON THE ISLAND OF TYSSØY, NORWAY, FOR CLOTHES TO MAKE A SCARECROW. SHE PLACED THEM OUTSIDE AND THE REMAINS WERE STILL VISIBLE 6 YEARS LATER. **LEFT:** THE 'COVER UP' COLLECTION FOR AUTUMN/WINTER 07/08 EXPLORED THE IDEA THAT THE RAINCOAT CAN ALSO BE WORN AS A PONCHO AND CAN BE BUTTONED TOGETHER WITH OTHER RAINCOATS TO MAKE TENTS. **ABOVE:** AN IMAGE OF A NORWEGIAN MOUNTAIN TAKEN BY STØLDAL ON HER MOBILE PHONE AS PART OF HER RESEARCH FOR THE 'COVER UP' COLLECTION.

STØLDAL'S work is characterized by a unique accidental quality. Playful yet carefully thought out, the designs apply traditional tailoring methods to unusual fabrics. Jackets are made from jersey cotton, bomber jackets from sleeping-bag material and sweatshirts are printed to look as though you are wearing a suit jacket and tie. *'I am inspired by how people use, wear and choose clothes,'* she explains. *'I find the relationship between people and their chosen attire fascinating, and each collection is based on research around these themes.'*

In previous collections, Støldal has looked into such themes as favourite clothes, dressing up and dressing down, sportswear and 'unconscious dressing' (a selected group of people was asked to make and dress a scarecrow). Støldal's memories of homemade clothes now worn out and discarded in her grandparents' attic have inspired much of her work. Clearly an instinctive storyteller, Støldal is occupied with the notion of a narrative. *'If I wasn't doing fashion then I would still somehow try to play with ideas. I would set myself briefs and somehow solve them.'*

A collection entitled 'Scribble' involved using children's drawings that were sent to her from England, Japan, Italy and Norway. The children were asked to depict a cool boy, a cool man and a cool old man. *'I wanted to see how children define cool and age, and I was interested to see whether they used different colours or shapes to depict the different themes.'* The result was a collection of multi-coloured, hand-knitted pieces and scribble prints that adorned baggy sweatshirts, T-shirts and jeans.

'The creative process is not easy, but always enjoyable,' believes Støldal, who suggests that the most enjoyable element is the research. *'My process involves photography, conversation and sculpture. Then, when the information gets translated into a collection, you work a bit "blind" at first, not knowing exactly where it is going. This can be a hard and doubtful time. Then suddenly things start clicking and making sense. This is exciting and to see garments in the end that you have not seen before is very rewarding.'*

ABOVE: A STILL FROM THE FILM CREATED BY THE ARTIST LEWIS RONALDS FOR STØLDAL'S AUTUMN/WINTER 07/08 'COVER UP' COLLECTION. *OPPOSITE:* THE PATTERNED AND CHAIN-CABLED HAND-KNITTED JUMPER, FROM THE 'COVER UP' COLLECTION, IS SHOWN WITH A HAT THAT HAS A TWIG FROM A TREE KNITTED INTO IT. *OVERLEAF, LEFT:* WORKING WITH STYLIST THOM MURPHY, STØLDAL LIKES TO COMMUNICATE THE NARRATIVE OF HER INSPIRATIONS; HERE, AN OUTDOOR LIFESTYLE. *OVERLEAF, RIGHT:* A SNAPSHOT OF STØLDAL'S STUDIO SHOWS A FRUIT BOWL, THE BOOK *LEVIATHAN* BY PAUL AUSTER AND AN ARTICLE ABOUT THE ARTIST SOPHIE CALLE.

Støldal believes in allowing room for her garments to EVOLVE NATURALLY and develop in their own time. She is inspired by MISTAKES AND ACCIDENTS and uses methods that allow this to happen, believing that it keeps the collections fresh and it is stimulating if the CLOTHES HAVE A LIFE OF THEIR OWN.

Despite Støldal's apparently relaxed approach to fashion design her tailoring training is essential to the success of her collections. *'It is my background and the skill that lies behind what I do. I have always regarded collections that communicate clearly a new, exciting and forward-looking idea to be successful.'*

Støldal's customers are individuals who pick up on her references. *'I sometimes get contacted by men who wear my clothes. They are often creative and tell me about their work. They have been artists, designers, graphic designers, students, stylists, musicians, art critics and curators.'* There follows an exchange of creative ideas, initiated by the clothes, that Støldal feels is very productive and exciting. Global brand Fred Perry has enlisted the designer's skills, and applied her signature photo prints both to Fred Perry track jackets and polo shirts.

As a woman designing menswear, Støldal is in the minority and is always very conscious that her clothes need to retain their masculinity. There is a fine line that can easily be crossed when dealing with contemporary menswear, so Støldal focuses her collections on traditional shapes while trying to tread new ground in the design process by creating clothes that are wearable but have a narrative behind their creation.

Modern menswear, says Støldal, is a good example of how, if something is left to itself for a while, with time and space to experiment, it will flourish. She now believes menswear is as significant as womenswear. She says there has been a big change in what is deemed acceptable for normal menswear. According to Støldal, menswear buyers used to think the market was divided into mutually exclusive segments – either formal or casual. But this is not the case any more, as innovative designers are being encouraged to offer alternative solutions for male dress codes. Støldal's intelligent and unique approach to design produces a mix of casual and formal clothing. Her particular skills lie in transforming and redesigning traditional styles that appear inherently modern.

Støldal presented her collection at MAN in 2007, an event sponsored by Topman and Fashion East. Inspired by her native Norway thick knits and wax suits, she produced a collection that hinted at the countryside but was designed with an urban twist. Støldal showed her trademark check shirts within the collection and the colour scheme of blue, burnt orange, grey, green and beige was true to her distinctive palette. In the same year, Støldal was awarded the Norwegian Designer of the Year and cemented her name as a contemporary and influential menswear designer.

SPASTOR

Spanish design team Spastor takes fabrics and shapes associated with womenswear and weaves them into masculine garments. SHARP CUTTING TECHNIQUES and CONTEMPORARY STYLING create INNOVATIVE MENSWEAR that communicates a fresh European aesthetic.

In 1995, Sergio Pastor Salcedo and Ismael Alcaina Guerrero, the two designers behind the Spanish label Spastor, founded and presented their first womenswear collection, commissioned for a fashion event in Barcelona. They have also presented in Madrid, where they won the L'Oréal Award for the best collection in 2001. In 2005, they showed their first menswear collection at Paris Menswear Fashion Week, entitled 'Kind of Man'.

OPPOSITE: PHOTOGRAPHY PLAYS A KEY PART IN COMMUNICATING SPASTOR'S BRAND. HERE, THE YOUTHFUL VISION OF THE 'KIND OF MAN' SPRING/SUMMER 05 COLLECTION IS ENDORSED THROUGH THE SPECIFIC CHOICE OF MODEL AND ENVIRONMENT. **RIGHT:** THE IMAGES CREATED TO ILLUSTRATE THE COLLECTIONS EMPHASIZE THE MODERNITY OF THE LABEL; THESE IMAGES OF HANDS INFORM THE 'KIND OF MAN' SPRING/SUMMER 05 COLLECTION.

SPASTOR

A clean, neutral colour palette and razor-sharp cutting techniques have come to define the clothes created for the **_SPASTOR_** label. Salcedo and Guerrero play with proportion and fit to create garments that question traditional and formal menswear shapes. Masculinity is addressed in surprising fabrics and soft colours that are more often associated with womenswear garments.

Spastor excel in promoting their design concepts through the medium of photography. The images they create to illustrate their collections endorse the modernity of the label. Their choice of models presents a contemporary vision of their menswear philosophy and ensures that their clothes are presented in directional formats that communicate their distinctly modern look

The design team behind Spastor have collaborated with various artists, for example, photographer Daniel Riera for the collective exhibition 'Arts & Lounge' at the Museu D'Art de Granollers in Spain in 1999. They worked with artist Joan Morey on several projects, including the 'STP' project commissioned by Luis Adelantado art gallery in 2001, and a project addressing the Venice Biennale in 2003.

Salcedo and Guerrero collaborated with photographer Marcelo Krasilcik on the images for their Spring/Summer 05 collection 'Kind of Man', and have contributed to the charity Designers Against AIDS by designing a T-shirt.

Spastor creates a contemporary wardrobe for the cosmopolitan man. By referencing feminine details in the garments, the menswear takes on a distinct aesthetic. A modern use of fabric and a lean silhouette are crucial to the success of the brand, which strives to offer alternative design proposals.

AN INITIAL DRAWING FROM THE DESIGN TEAM IS DEVELOPED TO CREATE A GARMENT FOR THE 'FROM BEHIND' SPRING/ SUMMER 07 COLLECTION.

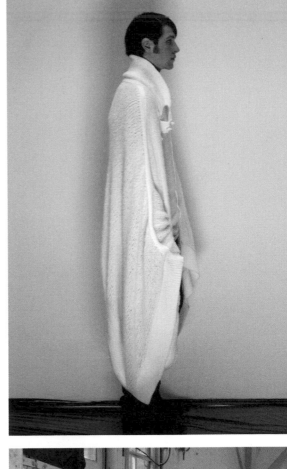

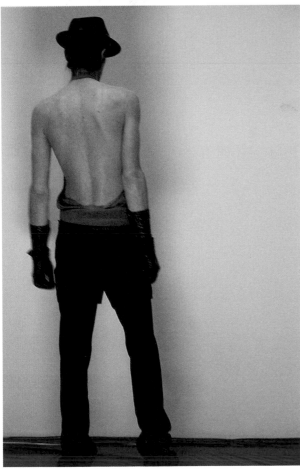

CLOCKWISE FROM TOP LEFT: A CATWALK SHOT FROM THE 'ARDE' SPRING/SUMMER 06 COLLECTION; A CATWALK IMAGE FROM THE 'GET INSIDE' AUTUMN/WINTER 05/06 COLLECTION; CLOTHES FROM THE 'KIND OF MAN' SPRING/SUMMER 05 COLLECTION; AND AN OUTFIT FROM THE 'GET INSIDE' AUTUMN/WINTER 05/06 COLLECTION. SPASTOR PRESENT THEIR SEASONAL COLLECTIONS AT THE PARIS MENSWEAR SHOWS.

1. *DESCRIBE YOUR DESIGN PHILOSOPHY.*

   'To make what we believe, what we feel, free and intense.'

2. *DEFINE YOUR AESTHETIC.*

   'We like very much what Frèderich Martin-Bernard said about us: Virile, sensual, and fragile with a strong character and a new free gentleman'.

3. *WHAT IS THE MOST REWARDING PART OF THE DESIGN PROCESS?*

   'The part when the collection starts to have its own structure, when we find the image of the collection, when we work with the garments, when we look for the figure, when the soundtrack sounds and when the whole concept is captured.'

4. *HOW WOULD YOU DESCRIBE YOUR MALE CUSTOMER?*

   'We like to think that there isn't only one Spastor customer. In Spain our customers range from eccentric aristocrats, to artists, young men and even women.'

5. *HOW WOULD YOU DESCRIBE THE PROCESS YOU GO THROUGH WHEN YOU DESIGN?*

   'It's quite a unique process; it never follows the same pattern and never comes about in the same way. Right now what nourishes us are our experiences, emotions, fears, myths, phobias, and of course the people we love, and the people we don't.'

6. *HOW WOULD YOU DEFINE SUCCESSFUL MENSWEAR?*

   'We believe that success is very subjective.'

7. *HOW IMPORTANT IS MASCULINITY FOR YOUR MENSWEAR DESIGNS?*

   'We think that masculinity has to do with the person, and not with the clothes.'

8. *WHO ARE YOUR DESIGN ICONS?*

   'Siouxsie Sioux, Ian Curtis, Klaus Nomi, Francis Bacon and Trent Reznor.'

9. *HOW WOULD YOU DESCRIBE CONTEMPORARY MENSWEAR?'*

   'We think that designers are beginning to explore and search for new ideas, and men are starting to enjoy them.'

10. *HOW DO YOU KNOW WHEN A GARMENT IS FULLY RESOLVED?*

    'To be honest, we don't know it. It has to do with intuition, and sometimes it is right, but sometimes it isn't.'

11. *WHAT IS THE MOST CHALLENGING ASPECT OF DESIGN?*

    'In our case, the lack of industrial and financial support.'

12. *HOW MUCH OF YOUR MENSWEAR IDEAS ARE BASED ON TRADITION?*

    'Tradition is a very important part of our menswear.'

13. *HOW CAN YOU BE INNOVATIONAL WITH MENSWEAR?*

    'Sometimes we consider ourselves to be very classical. One of our traits (even though we are not sure if this makes us innovative or modern) is that we use elements that are supposedly classical for women: fabrics, shapes, figures, endings and ways of sewing, and we apply them to menswear.'

OPPOSITE: THE 'FROM BEHIND' SPRING/SUMMER 07 COLLECTION SAW SPASTOR USE UNUSUALLY DARK COLOURS. PLAYING WITH PROPORTION AND FIT, SPASTOR MANIPULATED SOFT FABRICS TO CREATE THEIR DISTINCTIVE SIGNATURE STYLE.

STEPHAN SCHNEIDER

Citing traditional menswear as the basis of his design concepts, Stephan Schneider creates clothes for the ANTI-FASHION ESTABLISHMENT. His design philosophy is concerned with allowing the individual to be seen. HIS CLOTHES ALWAYS HAVE IMMACULATE QUALITY COMBINED WITH AN URBAN EDGE.

German-born Stephan Schneider graduated from the Royal Academy of Fine Arts in Antwerp, Belgium in 1994. Following the success of his final graduate collection, Schneider was awarded the opportunity to exhibit a stand of his work during Paris Fashion Week. He received several orders from international buyers and set his business up immediately.

OPPOSITE: SCHNEIDER OFTEN QUESTIONS AGE AND MASCULINITY IN HIS COLLECTIONS. THIS IMAGE IS FROM THE 'GROUP THEORY' COLLECTION, SPRING/SUMMER 01. **THIS PAGE:** YOUTHFUL VISION DEFINES SCHNEIDER'S STYLE, AND THIS IS EVIDENT NOT ONLY IN HIS GARMENTS BUT ALSO IN THE ACCOMPANYING FASHION IMAGERY THAT PROMOTES HIS COLLECTIONS. HE OFTEN REFERENCES YOUTH CULTURE, BOTH ITS ENVIRONMENTS AND ASSOCIATIONS. THIS SERIES OF IMAGES IS CALLED 'EVERY DAY IS LIKE YESTERDAY'.

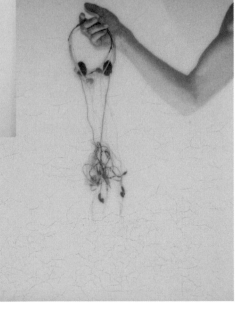

The company has grown steadily and _**SCHNEIDER**_ has more than 70 points of sale worldwide, his biggest market being Japan. In 1996, the first European flagship store was opened in the centre of Antwerp, and in February 2001 the flagship Tokyo store was opened. In 2007 Schneider was made professor of fashion at the University of the Arts in Berlin.

Schneider aims to dress the customer in a highly personal and recognizable way. Using the same fabrics for men and women, his collections present a man, who he describes, as a _'gentle character'_. The company uses its own production facilities in Belgian factories, where pieces are cut by hand and time is allowed for the finest finishing. Schneider presents distinctive pieces of clothing in a wide variety of fabrics to create an identifying and unequivocal look.

For his men's collections, Schneider is informed partly by his perceptions of age and masculinity. _'I think the most attractive element of a man is his boyishness, which some men never lose their whole life. My menswear wants to underline the boy in the man.'_ Schneider's youthful vision defines his style and is evident not only in the garments but also in the accompanying fashion imagery that promotes his collections. _'My philosophy can be described as continuation with passion,'_ explains Schneider. _'Good menswear should look effortless but still sophisticated and menswear shouldn't change drastically but it has to evoke strong feelings. My aesthetics are sort of a cheeky paradox around the borderline of sophistication and mass culture.'_

According to Schneider, contemporary menswear should be fresh and not overtly concerned with what is already established. His look is not about striving for perfection, as he believes garments should still look human and charming. _'It's important to stop in time,'_ he says. _'I don't change designs from prototype to prototype. I would rather give each piece a chance in its first version. The first garments often look less attractive as they are less refined. However they usually become more attractive the longer you see them. I often like the styles I don't like at the first view and then these always become my favourites when I see them hanging six months later in my stores.'_

The most enjoyable part of design for Schneider is when the end result is a surprise. _'The process of bringing a collection together doesn't always go very smoothly,'_ he states. _'But to imagine what it will become, what a tiny fabric swatch will look like as a finished garment or a proportion of a paper pattern later on the body is very exciting.'_

THIS PAGE: THE AFRICAN 'TOFU' COLLECTION, SPRING/SUMMER 05, SAW SCHNEIDER EXPLORE THE BOUNDARIES BETWEEN SOPHISTICATION AND MASS CULTURE. **OPPOSITE:** SCHNEIDER'S INTEREST IN THE CONCEPT OF BOYISHNESS IS SEEN IN HIS 'STORIES' COLLECTION FOR AUTUMN/WINTER 06/07.

Schneider believes that the most challenging part of the design process is to imagine. During the process of designing he has to imagine what colours, fabrics and proportions will look like in real garments. *'At the same time, I have to force myself to develop fabrics and patterns according to the fashion industry's metronome. I start each season by awaking a hunger in me. Sometimes it is a hunger for garments, colours or fabrics. In some collections there have been 15 different styles of shirts and in some collections there have been only three. This hunger for formality or hunger for fun creates the basic atmosphere for the season. Then I put a lot of effort into developing the fabric story. Ninety percent of the fabrics are my own design and colours. Then the volumes are fixed and the patterns made.'*

To see the finished collections and to be surprised by them season after season is still the best moment for Schneider. He derives pleasure from knowing that his clients, whom he describes as niche customers, will wear his garments. *'My customer doesn't see fashion as a status symbol. He is sort of an anti-fashion establishment and therefore not very brand minded. He wants to discover garments by himself and is not interested in the image of the name tag.'*

All menswear, Schneider maintains, is based on tradition. 'TRADITION MEANS CULTURE TO ME AND I DON'T REJECT IT. I don't see myself as an inventor and I don't see the quality in creating something totally new. I WOULD RATHER OBSERVE AND CREATE SOMETHING CONTEMPORARY.'

The designer's rapid creative and commercial success is proof that contemporary menswear that is presented in a progressive way can communicate and compete in a global market. As a teenager Schneider admits to having had sleepless nights over a Gaultier turtleneck, a Yamamoto suit and a John Flett jacket. As a designer, he has certainly found his true vocation. He explains, *'Since 1990, the moment I began my fashion studies, I had no more sleepless nights.'*

STEPHAN SCHNEIDER

VICTOR GLEMAUD

While still working in public relations, Victor Glemaud launched his energetic capsule collection of CASUAL DAYWEAR. His clever COLOUR COMBINATIONS acknowledge old-school styling and celebrate the pleasure in SUBTLE SIMPLICITY.

Born in Haiti in 1978, Victor Glemaud moved to the United States at the age of three, and was brought up in New York City. While still an undergraduate at the Fashion Institute of Technology (FIT) in New York, he began his career in fashion with an internship with American designer Patrick Robinson, who had previously worked for Anne Klein and then Calvin Klein. In 1998, while still at college, Glemaud took up the post of design assistant for Robinson.

OPPOSITE: IN HIS AUTUMN/WINTER 07/08 COLLECTION, THE V-NECK SWEATER WAS THE SIGNATURE PIECE. *RIGHT:* BRIGHTLY COLOURED GARMENTS AND SIMPLE SHAPES DEFINE GLEMAUD'S CONTEMPORARY MENSWEAR. THIS OUTFIT IS FROM THE AUTUMN/WINTER 07/08 COLLECTION.

VICTOR GLEMAUD

In 2000, **_GLEMAUD_** graduated from FIT and was hired as a publicist at fashion public relations company KCD based in New York. He worked on a range of men's and women's brands, including Versace, Marc Jacobs and Alexander McQueen.

After relocating to Paris in 2005, Glemaud went back to design for his mentor Patrick Robinson, who had taken over as artistic director of Paco Rabanne. Glemaud became a design adviser at Paco Rabanne and was responsible for the development of initial design concepts, global trend research and brand imaging. It is through these wide experiences of the fashion industry that Glemaud has built the foundation and deep knowledge that has been crucial to the successful launch of his own menswear collection, which debuted in 2006.

Glemaud's first collection was to set the tone for his label. Influenced by SCHOOL-BOY STYLES, Glemaud also established a BOLD USE OF COLOUR, which was DISTINCT AND CONFIDENT. His signature layered look featured two-tone cardigans made from one piece. Long johns in shades of grey with coloured ribbon down the sides were created to support the sweater-focused collection. Glemaud did not have the finances to produce the finely tailored trousers that he wanted, so he used the long johns as a WITTY AND ECONOMICAL substitute.

Abstract design concepts do not fuel Glemaud's inspiration; instead he wants to make clothes that he would wear himself. He clearly appreciates how young, modern men want to dress and sees his clothes as a fresh option for contemporary dress. His experience in fashion public relations has provided Glemaud with a realistic view of the fashion industry. He is aware of what is commercially viable and fuses this with original design ideas that are simple and very wearable.

OPPOSITE: DETAIL FROM THE AUTUMN/WINTER 07/08 COLLECTION SHOWING GLEMAUD'S WOOLLY LEGGINGS TEAMED WITH HIS SIGNATURE V-NECK AND WHITE SHIRT. **ABOVE:** LAYERED KNITWEAR FROM THE AUTUMN/WINTER 07/08 COLLECTION AND CLEAN-CUT MODELS HELP TO ENHANCE GLEMAUD'S SHARP BUT LAID-BACK AESTHETIC.

1. DESCRIBE WHAT YOU DO.
   'I hope I allow young guys to enjoy dressing up.'

2. HOW WOULD YOU DEFINE YOUR AESTHETIC?
   'Elegant, charming, relaxed, colourful!'

3. WHAT IS THE MOST FULFILLING ASPECT OF YOUR JOB?
   'The finished garment turning out like the image you had in your head.'

4. HOW WOULD YOU DESCRIBE YOUR CLIENTS?
   'Very, very new.'

5. WHAT FUELS YOUR DESIGN PROCESS?
   'Honestly, I take what I can afford.'

6. DOES YOUR DESIGN ACTIVITY ALWAYS FOLLOW THE SAME PROCESS?
   'My collections are based on the way I like and see clothes. The process starts
   with what I would like to add to my wardrobe – with what's missing.'

7. HOW WOULD YOU DEFINE A SUCCESSFUL MENSWEAR DESIGNER?
   'One who sells clothes that people enjoy wearing.'

8. HOW IMPORTANT IS MASCULINITY IN MENSWEAR?
   'Very.'

9. WHO ARE YOUR DESIGN ICONS?
   'I wear Dries Van Noten, Brooks Brothers, Comme des Garçons, Versace,
   Lyle & Scott and Louis Vuitton.'

10. HOW MANY OF YOUR MENSWEAR IDEAS ARE BASED ON TRADITION?
    'My foundation is very classic. I like to mix in charming yet odd
    elements that give you something different.'

11. HOW DO YOU DESCRIBE CONTEMPORARY MENSWEAR?
    'Something that is open to new ideas.'

12. HOW DO YOU KNOW WHEN A GARMENT IS 'COMPLETE'?
    'I don't think they ever are.'

13. WHAT IS THE MOST CHALLENGING ASPECT OF DESIGN?
    'Selling it!'

FOR HIS SPRING/SUMMER 07 COLLECTION, GLEMAUD LAYERED
CLASSIC GARMENTS IN SIMPLE SHAPES TO GIVE A MODERN AND
RELAXED FEEL.

VICTOR GLEMAUD

VIKTOR & ROLF

Since their couture debut, Viktor & Rolf have stunned the fashion industry with their WITTY CREATIVITY. Their menswear collections have successfully mellowed their artistry to a SYNTHESIS BETWEEN CREATIVITY AND DESIRABLE CLOTHES. The Monsieur label has extended the design team's international appeal.

Viktor & Rolf are Viktor Horsting and Rolf Snoeren. They were both born in 1969 in The Netherlands, and they formed their partnership whilst studying fashion design at the Arnhem Academy of Art in their home country. After graduating in 1992, they moved to Paris to develop their design concepts and undertook internships at Maison Martin Margiela and Jean Colonna.

FOR THEIR AUTUMN/WINTER 05/06 COLLECTION, VIKTOR & ROLF PRESENTED A NEW EMPHASIS ON COMMERCE, RATHER THAN HIGH CONCEPT. INSPIRED BY DUTCH NAVAL HISTORY, THE DUO SHOWED WEARABLE CLOTHING WITH SUCH DETAILS AS SUBTLE RUCHING ON SHIRTS, A TURNED-UP CUFF ON A JACKET SLEEVE OR A DOUBLE CUFF ON A SHIRT.

In 1993, **_VIKTOR & ROLF_** won the prize for fashion at the Hyères International Festival of the Arts and Fashion in the south of France. With this came an invitation to present their first haute-couture collection at Paris Fashion Week in 1998. They became the first and only Dutch guest members of the Chambre Syndicale de la Couture Parisienne, which organizes and monitors haute couture.

Although Viktor & Rolf received acclaim for their visionary clothes, they became just as famous for not selling any. Art galleries showed the first interest in their concepts, before the fashion industry fell for their charm. Richard Martin, then curator of New York's MoMA's Costume Institute, declared, *'The hybrid of art and fashion that Viktor & Rolf so uniquely make cannot be measured against art or fashion alone.'*

Viktor & Rolf flyposted the streets of Paris in 1996 to announce their own strike. It was an act of rebellion against the pressure to create a new collection every six months. In 2000, they launched a women's ready-to-wear line that appropriated America's stars and stripes to emphasize their commercial motivation to sell clothes. The success of the collection proved the team could be creative and sell clothes simultaneously.

The Fashion Museum in Paris presented a ten-year retrospective of Viktor & Rolf's work in 2003. In 2005, they opened their first flagship store in the Golden Triangle (Quadrilatrero d'Oro) in Milan and developed their first perfume, called Flowerbomb. In 2006, their first fragrance for men, Antidote, was introduced. In the same year, they followed Karl Lagerfeld and Stella McCartney in designing a line for the Swedish-based retailer Hennes & Mauritz (H&M).

Viktor & Rolf have also worked as curators for several exhibitions, and have designed stage outfits for several theatre productions. It was through these artistic visions, channelled into concept-driven catwalk presentations, that the design team gained notoriety in the fashion industry. Their creation of the 'atomic bomb' in 1998 was a combination of extreme fashion and art, achieved by stuffing necklines with silk party decorations including balloons and festoons. All the designs were shown twice: first in *'blown-up'* form, and then without the colourful stuffing when they appeared empty and oversized. In 2001, their all-black collection, called 'Black Hole', was presented on models whose faces, hands and legs were painted black.

As a springboard for their avant-garde fashion designs, Viktor & Rolf's fashion shows set out to *CHALLENGE TRADITIONAL METHODS OF FASHION COMMUNICATION*. Their shows are akin to *THEATRE PERFORMANCES* with the associated trappings of *ACTORS, MUSIC AND DANCING*. As *PURE FANTASY* their presentations became as infamous as the clothes they designed.

AS ARCH ILLUSIONISTS VIKTOR HORSTING AND ROLF SNOEREN RARELY MISS AN OPPORTUNITY TO BE THE CENTRE OF ATTENTION IN THEIR OWN COLLECTIONS. HERE, THEY MODEL GARMENTS FOR THEIR MONSIEUR AUTUMN/WINTER 04/05 COLLECTION.

VIKTOR & ROLF

ABOVE: VIKTOR & ROLF CITED MAGIC AS THE INSPIRATION FOR THEIR SPRING/SUMMER 05 COLLECTION. *RIGHT AND ABOVE RIGHT:* 'COSMOPOLOCAL' WAS THE NAME GIVEN TO VIKTOR & ROLF'S AUTUMN/WINTER 07/08 COLLECTION. THE CONCEPT WAS BASED ON THE DIVERGENCE BETWEEN THE CITY AND THE COUNTRY. ALL OUTFITS WERE PAIRED WITH TRADITIONAL BRIGHT YELLOW DUTCH CLOGS TO ENDORSE THE DIFFERENCES BETWEEN FOLK AND COSMOPOLITAN DRESS CODES.

The Viktor & Rolf store in Milan adheres to the design team's quirky take on clothes presentation. The entire store is based around the idea of being upside down, with only the clothes hanging the correct way. Chairs, the carpet, a fireplace and even the logo are turned upside down to create a theatrical environment. The surrealistic world was designed by architect Siebe Tettero, who worked with the two designers on their new headquarters in Amsterdam. His brief was based on their desire to offer a new perspective on shop design.

Their womenswear aesthetic is inherently modern, with a focus on extreme layering, dramatic shapes and volume. Their clothes explore distortion, exaggeration and the repetition of classical design shapes and elements. As expert cutters and drapers, Viktor & Rolf successfully subvert and twist the conventions of couture to produce new and exciting contemporary visions.

For instance, in 2002 their 'Blue Screen' show projected images onto bright blue garments, transforming the models into walking special-effects screens. *The New York Times Magazine* described Viktor & Rolf as *'artists, and fashion is their medium'*. Other theatrics have included enlisting a model to wear large, porcelain accessories, which were then ceremoniously smashed on the floor. In their 'Babushka' show in 2002 they dressed a model in ten layers of couture dresses, piled on top of one another, then placed her on a revolving plinth and undressed her layer by layer. In 2000, they learned to tap dance so they could take centre stage in their own show's finale. Their collections have also featured several performers including Tilda Swinton, Tori Amos and Rufus Wainwright.

Viktor & Rolf presented their first menswear collection in 2003. They called the line 'Monsieur', and for their presentation they modelled the clothes themselves, changing outfits on the stage. Since then, their menswear collections have been visualized in equally conceptually driven presentations. In 2006, for their winter collection, they were inspired by the magician Houdini. Suit jackets were adorned with straight white lines and neckties were given microscopic lines designed to trick the eye. And, as a link with Houdini, the great escape artist who wore chains and padlocks, Viktor & Rolf used the same motifs, with tiny chains and padlocks featuring as accessories.

Despite their concept-driven shows, Viktor & Rolf create menswear that always presents a modern immediacy. The success of the clothes lies in the charm of the presentation and the innate ability to fuse wit with contemporary, desirable clothes.

Viktor & Rolf have successfully created a menswear brand that is a REFLECTION AND EXTENSION OF THEIR OWN IMAGE. They have used their DISTINCT IDENTITY and translated it into viable clothing. By keeping their menswear AESTHETIC STRAIGHTFORWARD, Viktor & Rolf create clothes that appeal to a wide audience and allow the wearer to participate in the Viktor & Rolf RADICAL VISION.

VIVIENNE WESTWOOD

Putting men in skirts was only the tip of the iceberg for Vivienne Westwood's UNCOMPROMISING VISION of contemporary menswear. Her clothes fuse street style with traditional tailoring. HUMOUR is always apparent in a Westwood collection and a POLITICAL MESSAGE is never far from the agenda. WESTWOOD'S APPEAL IS HUGE AND HER CREATIVITY IMMENSE.

Vivienne Westwood is often described as the most creative, provocative and influential British designer. As a person and as a brand, Vivienne Westwood has inspired designers for decades with her iconic style. Her success as a designer has seen her rise from shop-owner to the founder of an influential global fashion company. She has been awarded an OBE by Queen Elizabeth II for her contribution to British fashion and continues to inspire generations of up-and-coming designers.

OPPOSITE: FOR HER AUTUMN/WINTER 06/07 COLLECTION, WESTWOOD DECLARED THAT *'BRITAIN MUST GO PAGAN'*, AND SENT HER WHITE-FACED MODELS DOWN THE CATWALK DRESSED IN KILTS, BAGGY TARTAN TROUSERS AND FUR CLOAKS. *RIGHT:* A PROMOTIONAL SKETCH FOR THE VIVIENNE WESTWOOD COLLECTION.

LEFT: WESTWOOD IS WELL KNOWN FOR SUBVERTING CLASSIC BRITISH TAILORING TO CREATE CONTEMPORARY GARMENTS THAT ARE ROOTED IN TRADITION. THIS OUTFIT IS FROM THE AUTUMN/ WINTER 04/05 COLLECTION. *BELOW:* RICH OPULENT COLOURS, AS IN THIS OUTFIT FROM THE SPRING/SUMMER 04 SEASON, HAVE BECOME A SIGNATURE COMPONENT OF WESTWOOD'S COLLECTIONS. *RIGHT:* WESTWOOD'S MENSWEAR NEVER SHIES AWAY FROM THE PROVOCATIVE; TIGHT-FITTING GARMENTS OFTEN DEFINE AND CELEBRATE THE MALE PHYSIQUE. ANDREAS KRONTHALER, WESTWOOD'S HUSBAND, WEARS AN OUTFIT FROM THE 'ACTIVE RESISTANCE PROPAGANDA' COLLECTION, SPRING/SUMMER 06.

Born in 1941 in Derbyshire, England, **_WESTWOOD_** first became famous through her partnership with Malcolm McLaren, manager of The Sex Pistols. Together they invented the punk uniform from their World's End shop in London's Chelsea. Westwood's talent for being ahead of her time runs throughout her career. Creating her own concepts, from punk to new romantics and pirates, Westwood ensures that her clothes are always controversial, sexy, avant-garde, provocative and unique.

Designing from her studio in Battersea, London, Westwood works with a team of 30 designers to create the 'Westwood' look. It is noticeable that any Vivienne Westwood garment has little consideration for current trends as each piece is reflective of Westwood's belief that individuality is a value that ought to be encouraged.

'I think in the case of English men, they are more adventurous than women,' says Westwood. 'I used to work in my shop in World's End, and if a man and a woman came in together and were shopping for him – well, he'd choose something and she'd persuade him to put it back. In general, men are more adventurous in England.'

It is because of this belief in men's openness to new ideas that Westwood created the MAN label. Designed for the man who is fashion conscious and enjoys a new take on classic designs, the collection is created in Milan. Andreas Kronthaler, Westwood's husband, is the main collaborator on the label and his role is to bring a masculine essence to the Westwood style. 'My clothes allow someone to be truly individual, which goes against the thinking at the moment,' explains Westwood, 'If everybody is wearing the same thing, they are bound to look the same. The majority of people on the street look quite dreadful. They are lazy in their dress and take no time to express themselves through clothes. Minimalism in dress is a dominant force because people are so afraid of committing an error in taste in their clothes.'

In celebrating her heritage, Westwood is correctly described as a very British designer. 'I am English, and so it is impossible for me to ignore British culture in my designs.' The fabrics she uses are often traditional British fabrics – English flannel and barathea wool, Irish linen and Scottish tartan. These fabrics benefit from classic British manufacturing techniques, as represented by the Savile Row tradition. Westwood's menswear garments are renowned for challenging traditional shapes and pieces. She has no issue with dressing men in skirts or unconventional pieces; she explores masculinity and retains a contemporary edge.

For Westwood, customers are the best ambassadors for her clothes. When people discover them she believes they acquire an edge. *'My clothes are uncompromising in the sense that they are what they are, and are not trying to sell themselves to you. If you want them, they make you incredibly strong. But they are not asking you to want them. You have to decide, "yes that's what I am going to have". And when you wear them they say about you, "I'm something to be reckoned with. Take it or leave it". They allow you to project your personality, and are quite theatrical in the sense that they are real clothes, well designed, but they give you a chance to express yourself.'*

The design process, according to Westwood, is key to the success of a collection. She is firm in her belief that knowledge of technique has to be the starting point. *'Without technique, self-expression is impossible. The more you can have somebody teach you, the better. The more you will know. But at the end of the day, you have to do it for yourself. To find a way for yourself.'* Inspiration is also paramount, and the next step. *'The only place to find ideas is by looking at what people did in the past,'* she explains. *'It's the way you can be original. You can't be original by just wanting to do something. Nothing comes from a vacuum.'*

Westwood has always created a visual identity of controversy and rebellion. She is eager to involve young, up-and-coming photographers and to use new faces to front her campaigns.

The men's collections are designed as an EXTENSION to the Vivienne Westwood womenswear. They echo the design philosophy of the label, which is to be CONSISTENTLY PROVOCATIVE and EXCITING, encouraging the wearer to step outside the norm of masculine dress codes and EXPERIMENT WITH GARMENTS. Concepts of both masculinity and femininity are addressed in her outfits as Westwood pushes the boundaries of modern menswear design.

OPPOSITE: ORNATE LAYERING AND LUXURIOUS FABRICS IN DECADENT COLOURS WERE USED IN THE AUTUMN/WINTER 06/07 COLLECTION. ***THIS PAGE:*** INNOVATIVE CUTTING HAS ALWAYS BEEN A SIGNATURE OF WESTWOOD'S CLOTHES, AND SHE TRANSLATES THIS SKILL INTO HER MENSWEAR LABEL IN THESE OUTFITS FROM THE SPRING/SUMMER 04 COLLECTION.

VIVIENNE WESTWOOD

WALTER VAN BEIRENDONCK

Since 1983, Walter Van Beirendonck has PROVOKED the fashion industry with his AGGRESSIVE POST-PUNK VISIONS. A master of communication, Van Beirendonck packs his clothes with visual jokes, science fiction, logos, slogans, radical statements and cartoon characters.

Walter Van Beirendonck was born in 1957 in the Flemish town of Brecht in Belgium. In 1980, he graduated from the Royal Academy of Fine Arts in Antwerp, Belgium, and presented his first collection, 'Sado', in 1982. Along with five other Belgian designers and as part of the influential Antwerp Six, he achieved notoriety with his 'Bad Baby Boys' collection at the British Designer Show in London, 1987.

OPPOSITE: A PROMOTIONAL IMAGE FOR VAN BEIRENDONCK'S SPRING/SUMMER 89 COLLECTION, ENTITLED 'KING KONG KOOKS'. THE DESIGNER IS WELL KNOWN FOR PUSHING BOUNDARIES IN FASHION COMMUNICATION, AND HERE HE USED PHOTOGRAPHY TO PROMOTE HIS FASHION CONCEPTS. IMAGES WERE DESIGNED FOR MAXIMUM ENERGY AND IMPACT. **ABOVE:** 'LET'S TELL A FAIRY-TALE' COLLECTION FOR SPRING/SUMMER 87 EXPLORED THE DESIGNER'S HUMOROUS SIDE, WITH OVERSIZED GARMENTS USED TO PORTRAY A CHILDLIKE QUALITY. **RIGHT:** THE 'FUEL THE FIRE' SPRING/SUMMER 91 COLLECTION IS TYPICAL OF THE DESIGNER'S FASCINATION WITH USING BRIGHT COLOURS, CARTOON MOTIFS AND GRAPHICS.

'Loud, daring and innovative, but most of all very personal' is how *VAN BEIRENDONCK* describes his clothes. His collections always fuse a hedonistic mix of violence, comic culture, science fiction, safe sex and humour. Van Beirendonck's slogan *'Kiss the Future'* communicates the label's constant search for the new and the innovative.

W.&L.T. (Wild and Lethal Trash) was Van Beirendonck's breakthrough label, which he designed between 1993 and 1999. His shows became famous in Paris for their styling and for his progressive show concepts. The label's presentation was endorsed by contemporary and innovative communication, such as cutting-edge websites and CD-Roms.

'Since my first collections in 1985, I have always focused on menswear because I saw it as a challenge to design for a man,' explains Van Beirendonck. *'I introduced in later collections women's silhouettes, but designing for men always stayed a priority. I believe boundaries of men's fashion are far more "fragile" than in womens- wear. They are not that easy to change or stretch.'*

Changing boundaries is what Van Beirendonck aims to do. He rethinks conventions and continually questions beauty and traditional dress codes. Aside from this progressive thinking and experimenting, Van Beirendonck is also revered for his work with colours, prints, graphics and slogans. Azzedine Alaia once said, *'A Walter T-shirt expresses more than what others are expressing in a whole collection.'*

'I enjoy research, drawing and sketching, selecting fabrics and thread – the whole process. What I don't like is production.' Van Beirendonck describes how he becomes consumed in the design process. *'The process is very natural, when I have just finished a collection, I informally have already new points of interest to research, and than I get automatically into the next one. My design is usually the same. If I have the time I put my research in scrap- books, but if there is no time, it happens purely in my head and then I get straight to the sketching.'*

THIS PAGE: TIGHT-FITTING AND BRIGHT BODY-CONSCIOUS CLOTHES ARE KEY TO VAN BEIRENDONCK'S STYLE, WHICH OFTEN EXPLORES MASCULINITY AND SEXUALITY. THESE PIECES ARE TAKEN FROM THE 'FUEL THE FIRE' SPRING/SUMMER 91 COLLECTION. *OPPOSITE:* BELIEVING THE BOUNDARIES OF MEN'S FASHION TO BE MORE 'FRAGILE' THAN IN WOMENSWEAR, VAN BEIRENDONCK PLAYS WITH IDEAS OF YOUTH, AS SHOWN IN THIS PROMOTIONAL IMAGE FOR THE 'BAD BABY BOYS' AUTUMN/ WINTER 86/87 COLLECTION.

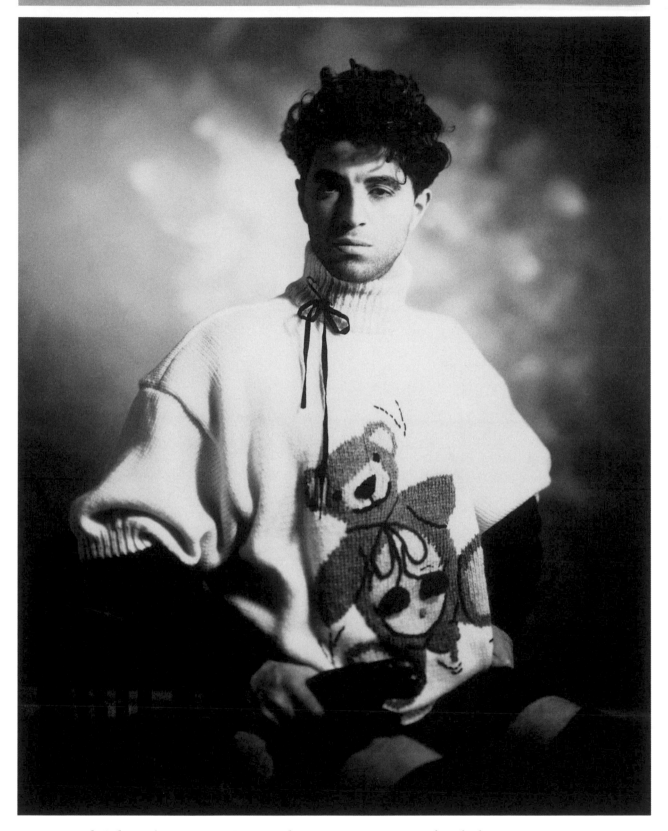

As one of Belgium's most PROLIFIC designers, Van Beirendonck has an APPETITE FOR KNOWLEDGE that fuels his designs, and society and contemporary incidents have a big influence on his work. 'I AM FASCINATED BY THE WORLD. I love to read and "surf" through books and libraries. I love art and exhibitions and I am amazed by the RITES, HABITS, CLOTHES and THE DECORATION of ethnic tribes.'

According to Van Beirendonck, his customer base is wide and varied. He describes a typical client as 'an open-minded, unconditioned person, man, woman or child, sensitive to colours and messages, to be different and adventurous.' Van Beirendonck's customers are loyal and they have grown to appreciate his attitude and philosophy. 'I wear my own designs and I combine these with military, vintage and also with fellow designers' clothes, such as Bernhard Willhelm.'

For Van Beirendonck, his men's collections are successful when there is a good balance between the new (not looking back/not retro), the wearable (should look 'natural', not fake) and the fresh (originality in colour, pattern and fabric). 'For me a garment, look or silhouette is finished when it reflects perfectly my signature, ideas and sketches,' he explains. Tradition is important in the sense of technique and skill. This, combined with a strong view towards the future, results in clear concepts. However, Van Beirendonck believes that tradition in the form of nostalgia is a waste of time.

'Masculinity is part of the game, but that's exactly why it is so interesting. In the "Gender? Collection" Spring/Summer 00, I questioned this matter and tried to figure out why gender and gender-related fashion is mainly dictated by society, the way we are raised and conditioned by the culture we are living in. Masculinity is important depending on the context and culture.'

Design icons include Pierre Cardin, Rei Kawakubo and Bernhard Willhelm, but Van Beirendonck believes that lately contemporary menswear is generally rather boring and repetitive, mainly concerned with selling and pleasing the widest target market.

To remain innovative and to constantly question what is going on in the men's fashion world is of paramount importance to Van Beirendonck. He is happy to attempt drastic changes and try out new directions. 'My independent way of working allows me to do this,' he says. 'The most challenging aspect of design is to create an immediate recognizable signature and creations with a timeless feel. I am still proud of pieces I created in 1985.'

Regularly collaborating with other artists and designers, Van Beirendonck also teaches at the Royal Academy of Fine Arts in Antwerp. He now designs exclusively for his own two labels: 'Walter Van Beirendonck' and 'aestheticterrorists'.

As a designer, Van Beirendonck continually questions the established rules in menswear, and his influence is still dominant today. As an integral member of the Antwerp Six, he has retained his young and challenging approach to creativity. His clothes have a distinct energy and are always bright, modern and provocative.

OPPOSITE: PORTRAIT OF VAN BEIRENDONCK TAKEN IN 1997. THE DESIGNER OFTEN APPEARS IN PROMOTIONAL IMAGES FOR HIS COLLECTIONS, AND HIS INDIVIDUAL STYLE HAS BECOME KEY TO THE SUCCESS OF THE BRAND. *ABOVE:* THE 'FETISH FOR BEAUTY' COLLECTION FROM THE WILD & LETHAL TRASH (W.&L.T.) LABEL FOR SPRING/SUMMER 98 COMMUNICATED THE DESIGNER'S ABILITY TO BOTH QUESTION AND CELEBRATE SEX AND SEXUALITY.

WALTER VAN BEIRENDONCK

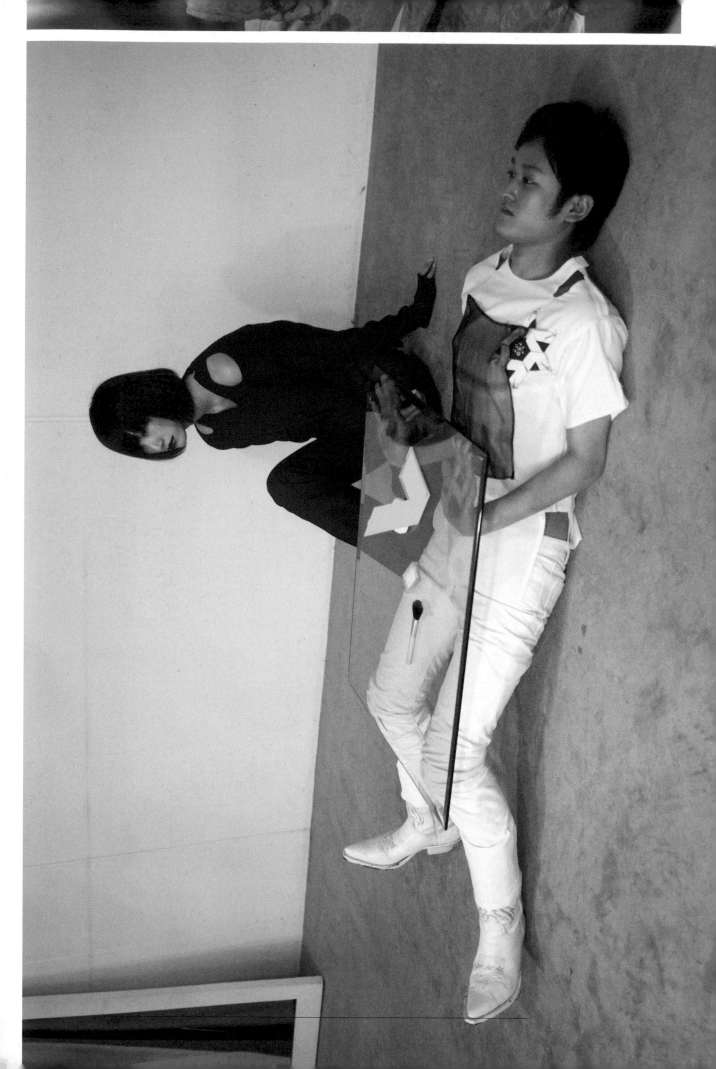

WENDY & JIM

With *CREATIVITY AND INNOVATION* as a focus, Wendy & Jim always communicate *FAR-REACHING VISIONS* through their clothes. Describing their style as 'DRY' and 'SLOW', they create each garment as part of an overall theme, which answers solely to an *AESTHETIC CONCEPT*. Installations and performances are key to their avant-garde philosophies.

The Vienna-based fashion label Wendy & Jim consists of designers Helga Schania and Hermann Fankhauser. Brought together in 1997 by their approach to fashion design, they are on a mission to suggest radical changes in dress. 'Our fuel is our work together. We talk with each other and discuss contemporary topics from the view of a fashion designer. Fashion is the language we speak the best, and with fashion we talk about everything.'

OPPOSITE: WENDY & JIM'S CONTRIBUTION TO A TOKYO EXHIBITION IN 2005 WAS ENTITLED 'HUMANE FURNITURE' AND INVOLVED THE DUO FUSING THEIR AVANT-GARDE CLOTHING CONCEPTS WITH IDEAS FOR FURNITURE PIECES. *RIGHT:* A PRINT DESIGN FOR A T-SHIRT FROM THE 'FAN OF WENDY & JIM' COLLECTION FOR SPRING/SUMMER 07.

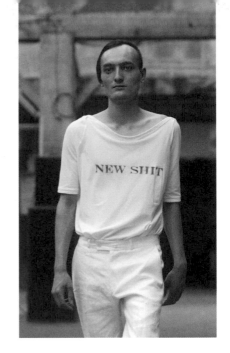

Both designers studied in the fashion department at the Institute of Design at the University of Applied Arts in Vienna, Austria, which was headed at the time by the legendary designer Helmut Lang. In 1999, they received substantial press at the Hyères International Festival of the Arts and Fashion in the south of France, which catapulted their brand to the attention of an international arena.

Since then, **_WENDY & JIM_** have been presenting their collections during Paris Fashion Week, and have been part of the official calendar there since their Spring/Summer collection 'Wiener Freiheit' in 2004. They describe their clothing as aggressive, modern and contemporary. _'Classic tailoring elements with avant-garde treatments, and also the opposite: avant-garde pieces in classical tailoring.'_ Their design is concerned with balancing creativity and reality. _'The most challenging aspect of design is not to be too avant-garde.'_

The team endeavours to discover NEW SHAPES and innovative ways of working with VOLUME. 'The words TIME and MODERN are very important in our work,' they explain. 'HEADING FORWARD AND BEING CURIOUS. Using unusual designs, prints, treatments on the patterns and clothes. Our look is MASCULINE, YOUNG and RADICAL.'

An appreciation of their traditional and influential environment is an important factor in their work. Vienna has a tradition of ceremonial clothes and Viennese balls, and the value of the classical has an impact on all forms of design including Viennese tailoring. _'This tradition plays a role in our unconsciousness as we design our menswear.'_ The team also recognizes Ralph Lauren as an inspirational design reference, believing he has created a hugely successful corporate identity.

Each crafted garment forms part of an overall theme and relates to an aesthetic concept. _'We start the working process by finding the right words and a working title for the collection – like "New Shit" or "Used Future", which helps us to collect ideas. The second step is to listen to certain music. This gives us the background for a twin-like cooperation, where we both have the same feeling for the collection and can work with the same goal in mind.'_ Although the starting process is very similar each season, the journey is different each time. _'The process then goes through a different landscape. It changes and is adjusted each season to what we are feeling.'_

OPPOSITE: INSPIRATIONAL IMAGES FOR THE 'USED FUTURE' COLLECTION, AUTUMN/WINTER 06/07. **_THIS PAGE:_** THE 'NEW SHIT' COLLECTION FOR SPRING/SUMMER 07 EXPLORED THE DESIGN TEAM'S SIGNATURE LOOK OF MASCULINE, YOUNG AND RADICAL CLOTHING.

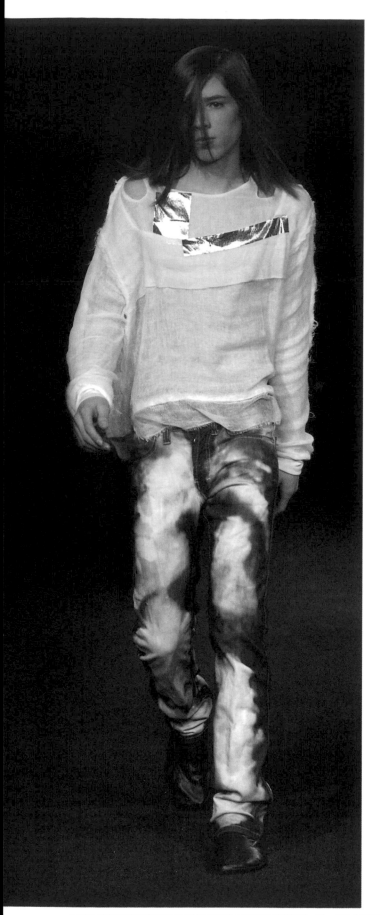

Wendy & Jim believe their customers are like themselves – eclectic – and they aim to make men feel good in their clothes.

'We get feedback from our customers that they receive many compliments about our clothes on the street.' Masculinity is also addressed in their work but the team does not have a rigid interpretation. 'Masculinity depends on the sign of the times. Sometimes masculinity is a big topic, sometimes femininity. It depends also on how you are going to interpret the masculine part of the collection.'

Presentations are known for being progressive and provocative. Their shows go to the heart of what they do. As they are trying to create a unique atmosphere for their work, they focus on every detail including the room, the music and the models. They work with stylists, photographers and even architects to get the right balance and effect. Usually, they avoid using professional models, instead opting for real people who can communicate a sensuality that is important to their collections.

Alongside their fashion presentations during Paris Fashion Week, Wendy & Jim also use installations and performances to convey their radical vision. These 'ideal settings' have been featured in a number of museums and exhibition areas worldwide. Since 2002, Wendy & Jim have invited artists, designers and other creative talents to quarter 21, an exhibition area in the Museums Quarter of Vienna for their project FOUND FOR YOU, which features fashion-related works, products and ideas.

Since 2003, Wendy & Jim have been guest members of the renowned Chambre Syndicale du Prêt-à-Porter des Couturiers et des Créateurs de Mode. Wendy & Jim garments are sold in cities all over the globe, including Hong Kong, Tokyo, Berlin, New York, Vienna and Stockholm.

Helga Schania and Hermann Fankhauser continue to work and live in Vienna and create inspirational alternatives for contemporary menswear. Their menswear collections communicate directly with those individuals who appreciate Wendy & Jim's devotion to conceptual clothing. Creativity is their language, and they express their ideas on contemporary menswear by challenging preconceived ideas about male clothing.

ABOVE: FOR THE 'USED FURNITURE' AUTUMN/WINTER 06/07 COLLECTION, WENDY & JIM USED UTILITARIAN BLEACHED DENIM. *OPPOSITE:* WENDY & JIM AVOID USING PROFESSIONAL MODELS FOR THEIR PRESENTATIONS, INSTEAD OPTING FOR REAL PEOPLE WHO CAN COMMUNICATE A SENSUALITY THAT IS IMPORTANT TO THEIR COLLECTIONS. THE IMAGES ARE TAKEN FROM THE 'MEMORIES-PIECES IN A MODERN STYLE' COLLECTION FOR SPRING/SUMMER 05.

WOODS & WOODS

YOUTHFUL BUOYANCY defines the aesthetic of Woods & Woods. With an IMMACULATE ATTENTION TO DETAIL, the label fuses sportswear shapes with an acute knowledge of traditional menswear garments. PROGRESSIVE AND INNOVATIVE, the brand presents an urban edge through a SHARP AND PRECISE SENSIBILITY.

Singaporean Jonathan Seow is the designer behind the label Woods & Woods. Born in 1977, Seow runs his international brand from Singapore. The label produces three collections – 'pour femme', 'pour homme' and 'femme plus' – all of which are sold across the globe.

OPPOSITE: THE CONTEMPORARY WHITE WOOL JACKET AND THE NYLON AND COTTON SHIRT ARE FROM WOODS & WOODS'S AUTUMN/WINTER 06/07 COLLECTION. **RIGHT:** JONATHAN SEOW, THE DESIGNER (IN ORANGE), MAKES ADJUSTMENTS TO THE GARMENTS ON THE MODELS DRESSED IN THE AUTUMN/WINTER 05/06 COLLECTION.

Seow studied fashion at Raffles Design Institute, Singapore and it was during his college years that he became fascinated by cutting the same garment in different fabrics. His obsession, and consequently his trademark, lies in the construction and finish of each garment, which remains the focus for his urban and edgy clothes.

In 1997, Seow went to work for Singapore's only other international brand, Song & Kelly. In 2001, he set up his own label entitled **_WOODS & WOODS_**, and since then he has showcased his seasonal collections in Seoul, Tokyo, Paris, Berlin, Hong Kong and Australia. He presented his first collection at the 'Who's Next' show in Paris in 2004. Subsequently, Woods & Woods went on to present its debut runway collection on the official calendar of the Paris Fashion Week for Men Spring/Summer 05. Seow's Autumn/Winter 06/07 collection was presented at 'IDEAL' during Berlin Fashion Week, and his Spring/Summer 07 collection was presented at 'Rendez-vous Femme' in Paris.

Seow has been selected for the finals of several prestigious award shows and exhibitions. For example, Osaka Fashion Grand Prix, Chic Chinois International Design Exhibition, Smirnoff International Fashion Awards, Asian Young Designers Award, iDN, ITS 2nd edition (International Talent Support by Diesel) and MittelModa 12th edition (by Camera Moda Nazionale Italiano).

Talking about his fashion design philosophy for menswear, Seow is clear about his objectives. *'I hope to push certain conventions, within the realm of fashion, which translate into a seemingly relaxed radicalness that exudes an unguarded elegance,'* he explains. This uncompromising approach to design and its execution has established Seow as a perfectionist in terms of quality and attention to detail.

Many design icons inspire Seow's aesthetic. He lists artist August Sander; designers Walter Van Beirendonck, Helmut Lang, Cristobal Balenciaga and Josephus Thimister; musicians The Smiths and David Bowie; and architect Santiago Calatrava as inspirational figures for his work.

OPPOSITE: THE WHITE PERFORATED KNIT CARDIGAN, NYLON AND COTTON SHIRT AND WHITE SLIM-FIT JEANS COMMUNICATE A MODERN, STREAMLINED SILHOUETTE FOR THE AUTUMN/WINTER 06/07 COLLECTION. *RIGHT:* BACKSTAGE AT PARIS FASHION WEEK A MODEL WEARS A CHEQUERED SILK SHIRT WITH PERFORATED-KNIT TRACK PANTS FROM THE SPRING/SUMMER 06 COLLECTION.

For Seow, the DESIGN PROCESS starts with him looking at DIFFERENT FABRICS, SURFACE FINISHES, WEIGHTS, OPACITIES, TEXTURES, COLOURS AND TOUCHES. 'The forms, volumes and details come after,' he says. 'Depending on what my influences are at that moment. After careful consideration, the COLLECTION'S ATMOSPHERE will take place NATURALLY somehow. MUSIC always fuels my design process, be it literally or not. I will always LISTEN TO MUSIC WHEN I AM INSPIRED.'

The anticipation before the completion of a collection is something Seow relishes. The preparation for a show, including model casting and line-ups, is immensely stimulating for the designer. 'There's always the expectancy of how a collection will look and feel as a whole with models, music, different show venues and atmospheres.' Seow is also driven by the process of thinking up new ideas for the next collection, which actually occurs while viewing the current collection backstage. The next season begins almost immediately. 'Watching the finale parade of a current collection is a very inspiring moment for me to glance forwards. There is always a rush.'

With a sensitive approach to his customers, Seow describes them as 'individuals who treasure a piece or garment that is close to its creator, as opposed to garments that exude an overly manufactured impression.' Seow is committed to balancing creativity with commercial viability, believing that successful menswear should be able to answer to its market at any time. This shows a deep understanding of how fashion and its markets are evolving. He affirms that a designer has to be progressive yet still able to retain a brand's philosophy and identity.

'Masculinity in menswear is the only thing that is able to set it apart from womenswear,' states Seow. 'There is still a fine line in between and I feel it should be preserved constantly.' He says that his work always aims to be articulate, modern and effortless at the same time. Recognizing when a garment is finished is also key to Seow's design philosophy. 'It is clear when a garment is complete, when adding any more will seem unnecessary and changes what you set out to design. A T-shirt should still be a T-shirt and when you finished making it, you know it's fully resolved.'

The most challenging aspect of design, Seow maintains, is finding the time to sit down and spend quality hours penning down all his thoughts and ideas, 'working out the construction of each piece that eventually leads to the realization of an actual garment in three-dimensional form. This somehow lends a sense of accuracy in the actual collection presented.'

Talking about balance in his work, Seow says, 'Fifty percent of my menswear design is based on tradition. I love the essence of a classic trench coat, bomber jacket, shirt and other generic items. In my opinion, this balance adds a good amount of sophistication and maturity in my work.'

Through his fabric applications, use of layering and styling, Seow aims always to remain innovative. By designing new details and re-working the fitting lines of classic menswear, Seow defines modern notions of menswear through the accompanying imagery and concepts.

In Singapore, Seow is a guest lecturer and consultant at the Fashion Institute of Singapore (FIOS), and is also the founder of 'Studio Privé', a project that houses and promotes the work of new Singaporean fashion designers.

Seow has successfully developed an international brand from a base in Singapore. His collections have global appeal through his contemporary interpretation of menswear design and its presentation.

ABOVE: WOODS & WOODS SPRING/SUMMER 05 CATWALK SHOW
WAS AT THE HOTEL ST. JAMES & ALBANY DURING PARIS FASHION
WEEK. A REVERSIBLE COTTON SWEAT AND A DENIM JACKET
WERE STYLED WITH GREY PINSTRIPE TROUSERS. *ABOVE RIGHT:*
MODELS LINE UP BACKSTAGE BEFORE THE SPRING/SUMMER 06
COLLECTION IS SHOWN AT PARIS FASHION WEEK. *RIGHT:*
BACKSTAGE AT THE SPRING/SUMMER 06 SHOW A MODEL WEARS
AN OFF-WHITE KNIT BLOUSON WITH DENIM SHORTS.

YOHJI YAMAMOTO

As master of the OVERSIZED SILHOUETTE, Yohji Yamamoto has changed fashion history. Expressing his UNIQUE PHILOSOPHY and AVANT-GARDE SPIRIT in his clothing, Yamamoto creates clothes that are distant from current trends. His craftsmanship-focused GARMENTS OFTEN WORK INDEPENDENTLY from the figure's contours and movement.

The only Japanese fashion designer to have been awarded the prestigious French Chevalier de l'Ordre des Arts et des Lettres (Order of Arts and Literature), Yohji Yamamoto was born in Tokyo in 1943. He studied law before attending the prestigious Bunka Fashion College in Tokyo. He presented his first womenswear collections in the early 1970s, and has since become a world-respected designer, winning the Mainichi Fashion Grand Prize in 1986 from the respected Japanese newspaper.

OPPOSITE: Y-3, THE COLLABORATION BETWEEN YAMAMOTO AND ADIDAS, HAS BEEN A HUGE COMMERCIAL SUCCESS DUE TO ITS INNOVATIVE FUSION OF SPORTSWEAR AND HIGH FASHION. THIS CATWALK IMAGE, FROM THE SPRING/SUMMER 07 COLLECTION, SHOWS YAMAMOTO'S CONFIDENT AND BOLD USE OF COLOUR. **BELOW:** FOR HIS AUTUMN/WINTER 04/05 COLLECTION, INSPIRED BY TEDDY BOYS, ROCKERS AND STREET GANGS, YAMAMOTO ASKED SUGGS AND HIS BAND MADNESS TO PERFORM ON THE RUNWAY. ACCORDING TO YAMAMOTO, HE WANTED TO SHOW THE REALITY OF ROCK'N'ROLL. **RIGHT:** A RED-AND-WHITE CHEQUERBOARD TRAINER FORM THE SPRING/SUMMER 07 Y-3 COLLECTION.

YAMAMOTO is highly regarded as a contemporary fashion thinker. He avidly expresses his avant-garde approach through his distinctive clothing, producing collections that are focused on abstract concepts. His clothes are characterized by oversized silhouettes, often featuring drapes and cutting-edge textures and fabrics.

In 1977, Yamamoto presented his first show in Tokyo. His debut women's collection was inspired by masculine garments, and the clothes were cut in bold shapes, washed fabrics and dark colours. The pieces communicated a functional elegance and abstinence that Yamamoto would re-establish years later in his menswear.

Along with Rei Kawakubo of Comme des Garçons and Issey Miyake, Yohji Yamamoto enhanced his design credibility in the 1980s by presenting a very different and challenging aesthetic on the Parisian catwalks. Their concepts were concerned with communicating different perceptions of fashion and beauty that had not been visualized before in the West.

In his first Paris show in 1981, Yamamoto set the tone for his progressive vision. The collection was described as 'pauperism' by the fashion press, for its use of dark tones, flat shoes and androgynous shapes. The look soon attracted a growing number of followers. Yamamoto's work became defined by his distinct use of black, highlighted with navy and white, and the occasional splash of colour. The extreme styles were sophisticated and often layered. The loose and flowing garments seemed like an anti-fashion statement in contrast with the established Parisian accentuated silhouette.

Designing for real Japanese women, Yamamoto explained that he was thinking of their comfort. 'Fashion is only complete when it is worn by ordinary people who exist now, managing their lives, loving and grieving,' writes Yamamoto in his book Talking to Myself. What Yamamoto did not comprehend at the time was that his style suggested a new approach to the body.

His clothing focused on the NEGATIVE SPACE BETWEEN THE BODY AND THE GARMENT rather than the actual body. The garments naturally changed with the figure's contours and movement. This DISTINCT DESIGN PHILOSOPHY was revolutionary.

ABOVE: FOR AUTUMN/WINTER 07/08, YAMAMOTO FUSED HIS FASCINATION WITH TAILORED EDWARDIAN SILHOUETTES WITH KNITWEAR INSERTS, COMBINING HARD AND SOFT FABRICS. RIGHT: YAMAMOTO HAS ALWAYS QUESTIONED THE IDEA OF AN ACCEPTABLE CODE OF MASCULINE DRESS. IN HIS SPRING/SUMMER 04 COLLECTION, HE PUT THE MODELS IN LONG SHIRTS THAT APPEARED LIKE DRESSES.

YOHJI YAMAMOTO

This new approach to clothing was also a comment on the post-industrial world that brought together ideas from the East and the West. He describes how he was inspired to produce clothes as a reaction to mass production, stating that people of his generation were ripped off by economic success. During his youth, the industry kept pumping out new products that they did not believe in because they knew, come tomorrow, they would be out of style. Yamamoto's was the first generation to wear second-hand clothes as a reaction to mass production.

Yamamoto's influence continues to INFIL TRATE CONTEMPORARY FASHION, and his menswear sets the same vision. He has succeeded in OVERTURNING ALL THE SET RULES of modern fashion. By rejecting traditional perceptions of beauty and glamour, Yamamoto has provided a platform for ALTERNATIVE AESTHETICS. He appeals to individuals who appreciate HUMOUR, ROMANCE and HISTORY IN FASHION. His collections often reference the past but they are always presented in a MODERN way.

It was in Paris in 1984 that Yamamoto launched his first menswear collection. He continued his conviction of presenting apparently simple garments with sophisticated construction techniques. His men's uniform often mixes British references, such as punk, with an Eastern spin. Pieces are often informed by wardrobe basics that are modernized through fabric and cutting techniques. Making subtle twists to classic garments provides men with utilitarian and contemporary wardrobe options. His clothing for men is neither masculine nor feminine. The garments are often described as transcending both time and culture.

In 2003, Yamamoto formed a partnership with sportswear label Adidas to create the Y-3 label, one of the first and most successful of the designer–active-wear unions. The collaboration brought sportswear to a contemporary fashion market, and vice versa. The modern design appealed to a wide audience and Y-3 has been a huge financial success. The requirements of athletic wear seem to fuse well with the utilitarian aspects of Yamamoto's designs. Although the Y-3 logo is emblazoned on the garments, the voluminous proportions and minimal colour palette of black, white, navy and red are true to Yamamoto.

Yamamoto signed a deal to design luggage and accessories for Italian luggage specialist Mandarina Duck in 2006. Not only does Yamamoto dress a large majority of the international arts community, he has also collaborated on film projects with directors Wim Wenders and Takeshi Kitano and musician Ryuichi Sakamoto. Furthermore, he has created costumes for the Pina Bausch dance company and the Wagner Opera, both in Germany.

Yohji Yamamoto is considered to be one of the most influential designers working today. As a conceptually driven visionary, he creates clothes that are often intellectual and sometimes difficult to understand. As he fuses the classic with the avant-garde, his clothes become almost abstract. They avoid communicating a distinct personality and therefore appeal to a wide and diverse range of customers.

OPPOSITE: A BELT FROM THE Y-3 SPRING/SUMMER 07 COLLECTION. *ABOVE LEFT:* MIXING SPORTSWEAR AND FORMAL FABRICS FOR AUTUMN/WINTER 03/04, YAMAMOTO PRESENTED A COLLECTION THAT EXPLORED FUNCTIONAL DETAILS AND TRADITIONAL FORMAL SHAPES. *ABOVE:* FOR THE AUTUMN/WINTER 06/07 SEASON, YAMAMOTO SHOWED HIS SIGNATURE NAVY AND BLACK IN A GOTHIC-INSPIRED COLLECTION. *LEFT:* YAMAMOTO OFTEN USES OLDER MEN IN HIS PRESENTATIONS AS HE DOES NOT PRESCRIBE TO THE STEREOTYPICAL CONNOTATIONS OF MALE MODELS. THESE GARMENTS ARE FROM THE AUTUMN/WINTER 04/05 COLLECTION. *BELOW:* A SKETCH FROM ONE OF YAMAMOTO'S EARLY MENSWEAR DESIGNS ILLUSTRATES THE BOXY SILHOUETTE THAT HAS COME TO DEFINE HIS STRUCTURAL GARMENTS.

YOHJI YAMAMOTO

PICTURE CREDITS

COVER: PHOTOGRAPHY PLATON
P. 1: PHOTOGRAPHY CLAIRE ROBERTSON
P. 2: PHOTOGRAPHY IVANHO HARLIM
P. 3: PHOTOGRAPHY TAKAY AT JED ROOT
P. 4: PHOTOGRAPHY PATRICK ROBYN
PP 5 AND 6: PHOTOGRAPHY GREGOR HOHENBERG
P. 8: PHOTOGRAPHY TRINE GULDAGER
P. 9: PHOTOGRAPHY RONALD STOOPS

AITOR THROUP
P. 12: PHOTOGRAPH FROM *i-D* MAGAZINE, FEBRUARY 2007.
PHOTOGRAPHY NICK BROWN, STYLING AND ART DIRECTION
AITOR THROUP. (CLOTHING CREDITS: BASEBALL CAP TOPMAN;
RED JACKET JIL SANDER; SHOES BUDDAHOOD; SILVER JACKET,
RED BEAD-BAG TIE, SHIRT, 3-D TWIST TROUSERS WITH FEET
AND WHITE MESH SCULPTURE ALL AITOR THROUP.)
PP 12–13: LINE-UP DRAWING FROM EVISU COMPETITION,
'FIGHTING COUNTERFEIT THROUGH DESIGN', RCA, 2005.
P. 15, BACKGROUND: PHOTOGRAPH OF AITOR THROUP'S STUDIO
BY JEZ TOZER, 2007; FOREGROUND: PHOTOGRAPH OF 6-HOODED
'SKANDA' JACKET FROM 'WHEN FOOTBALL HOOLIGANS BECOME
HINDU GODS', RCA, 2006.
P. 16: PROMOTIONAL DRAWING BY AITOR THROUP FOR MAN,
LFW FEBRUARY 2007.
PP 16–17: BACKGROUND PROFILE LINE-UP PHOTOGRAPH OF
MA COLLECTION, 'WHEN FOOTBALL HOOLIGANS BECOME
HINDU GODS', 2006. PHOTOGRAPHY ROSS WILLIAMS. (CLOTHING
CREDITS: FOOTWEAR BY MARK EMMETT FOR AITOR THROUP;
BASEBALL CAPS/MASKS BY AITOR THROUP AND PRODUCED BY
RIZVI MILLINERY.)
P. 17, BOTTOM RIGHT: SKULL-SHAPED MILITARY BAGS BY AITOR
THROUP, PRODUCED BY RIZVI MILLINERY, FROM 'WHEN
FOOTBALL HOOLIGANS BECOME HINDU GODS'.

ALEXANDER McQUEEN
ALL PHOTOGRAPHY MITCHELL SAMS

BLAAK
ALL PHOTOGRAPHY TAKAY AT JED ROOT

BURBERRY
P. 36: PHOTOGRAPHY PERRY HAGOPIAN
PP 34, BOTTOM AND 35, FRONT: PHOTOGRAPHY MITCHELL SAMS
P. 34, TOP AND LEFT: PHOTOGRAPHY CATWALKING.COM

BERNHARD WILLHELM
PP 22 AND 23: PHOTOGRAPHY CATWALKING.COM
PP 24 AND 25: PHOTOGRAPHY MITCHELL SAMS

COSMIC WONDER LIGHT SOURCE
PP 38 AND 41: © COSMIC WONDER
P. 39, LEFT: © YUKINORI MAEDA
P. 39, RIGHT: © COSMIC WONDER JEANS
P. 40, LEFT: © COSMIC WONDER SHOP
P. 40, RIGHT COLUMN: © COSMIC WONDER LIGHT SOURCE

DIOR HOMME
P. 52: PHOTOGRAPHY ALICE HAWKINS
PP 53 AND 55: PHOTOGRAPHY MITCHELL SAMS
P. 54: PHOTOGRAPHY PERRY HAGOPIAN
P. 56: PHOTOGRAPHY MITCHELL SAMS
P. 57: PHOTOGRAPHY PAULA KUDACKI

DRIES VAN NOTEN
PP 58, 58–59 AND 60–61: PHOTOGRAPHY CATWALKING.COM
PP 59, LEFT AND RIGHT AND 60–61, BOTTOM BAND:
PHOTOGRAPHY MITCHELL SAMS

DSQUARED2
P. 48: PHOTOGRAPHY © JASON EVANS

DUCKIE BROWN
ALL PHOTOGRAPHY PLATON

FRANK LEDER
ALL PHOTOGRAPHY GREGOR HOHENBERG
ALL IMAGES © FRANK LEDER

GASPARD YURKIEVICH
PP 74, 76, 77, 78 AND 79: PHOTOGRAPHY SHOJI FUJII
P. 75: PHOTOGRAPHY ALFREDO SALAZAR
ALL IMAGES © GASPARD YURKIEVICH

JOHN GALLIANO
PP 84, 88 AND 89: PHOTOGRAPHY PATRICE STABLE
PP 85, 86 AND 87: © JOHN GALLIANO HOMME

JOSEP ABRIL
PP 90 AND 94: CONCEPT AND DESIGN ALESSIA ZOPPIS;
PHOTOGRAPHY CARLES A. ROIG
PP 91, 92 AND 95: PHOTOGRAPHY CARLES A. ROIG,
WWW.LARETRATERIA.COM

KIM JONES
P. 96: *DOINGBIRD MAGAZINE*, ISSUE 9, STYLING JOE McKENNA,
PHOTOGRAPHY ALASDAIR McLELLAN
P. 97: PHOTOGRAPHY KIM JONES
P. 98: EMBROIDERY © KIM JONES 2007
P. 99, TOP LEFT: PHOTOGRAPHY CATWALKING.COM
P. 99, TOP RIGHT: PHOTOGRAPHY OSCAR CHANG-ANDERSON.
PRODUCED FOR KIM JONES BY AND WITH PERMISSION FROM
OSCAR CHANG-ANDERSON TO BE REPRODUCED IN *MODERN
MENSWEAR*. © OSCAR CHANG-ANDERSON/KIM JONES 2007

MAISON MARTIN MARGIELA
PP 100 AND 103: PHOTOGRAPHY JACQUES HABBAH
P. 102: PHOTOGRAPHY RONALD STOOPS
P. 104: PHOTOGRAPHY OLA RINDAL

MARC JACOBS
PP 106, FRONT AND 107: PHOTOGRAPHY PERRY HAGOPIAN
PP 106, BACK, 108, TOP AND 111: © MARC JACOBS, AUTUMN/
WINTER 06/07
PP 108, BOTTOM AND 110: © MARC JACOBS, SPRING/SUMMER 07
P. 109: PHOTOGRAPHY CATWALKING.COM. © MARC JACOBS,
SPRING/SUMMER 96

MEADHAM/KIRCHHOFF
PP 113 AND 116, RIGHT: PHOTOGRAPHY ALISTAIR GUY
P. 115: PHOTOGRAPHY CLAIRE ROBERTSON

PATRIK SÖDERSTAM
PP 120–21: PHOTOGRAPHY MAGNUS CARLSSON
ALL OTHER IMAGES AND ARTWORK BY PATRIK SÖDERSTAM

PAUL SMITH
PP 124–25: © NORBERT SCHOERNER WWW.CLMUK.COM
P. 126: PHOTOGRAPHY CATWALKING.COM
P. 128: PHOTOGRAPHY LANCE CHESHIRE

PETER JENSEN
P. 130: PHOTOGRAPHY MAURO COCILIO
P. 131: PHOTOGRAPHY ABÄKE, MAKE-UP ALEX BOX
PP 132–33: PHOTOGRAPHY TIM GUTT, STYLING SHONA HEATH
P. 133, RIGHT: ILLUSTRATION BY ALEX FOXTON
P. 134, BORDER IMAGE: PHOTOGRAPHY CATWALKING.COM
P. 134: PHOTOGRAPHY PAUL BLISS, STYLING MATTIAS KARLSSON
P. 135: PHOTOGRAPHY DENNIS SCHOENBERG

RAF SIMONS
PP 137 AND 138–39: PHOTOGRAPHY CATWALKING.COM
PP 140 AND 141: PHOTOGRAPHY ANNICK GEENEN
P. 141, BORDER IMAGE: PHOTOGRAPHY MITCHELL SAMS

RICK OWENS
PP 142, BACK, 143, 144, 145 AND 146, FAR RIGHT:
PHOTOGRAPHY RICK CASTRO
PP 142, FRONT, 146 INTERIOR PHOTOGRAPHS AND 147:
PHOTOGRAPHY OWENSCORP

SIV STØLDAL
PP 148 AND 149, RIGHT: PHOTOGRAPHY SIV STØLDAL
PP 149, LEFT, 151 AND 152: PHOTOGRAPHY TOPSHOP
PP 150–51: PHOTOGRAPHY LEWIS RONALD
P. 153: PHOTOGRAPHY TRINE GULDAGER

SPASTOR
P. 154: PHOTOGRAPHY MARCELO KRASILCIC, © SPASTOR
P. 155: PHOTOGRAPHY MARCELO KRASILCIC AND
WADE H. GRIMBLY, © SPASTOR
P. 157, TOP ROW: PHOTOGRAPHY WADE H. GRIMBLY, © SPASTOR
P. 158: PHOTOGRAPHY BIEL SOL, © SPASTOR

STEPHAN SCHNEIDER
P. 160: PHOTOGRAPHY ROGER DIJCKMANS
P. 161: PHOTOGRAPHY KIRA BUNSE; ART DIRECTION
CHEWING THE SUN
PP 162 AND 163: PHOTOGRAPHY KIRA BUNSE

VICTOR GLEMAUD
PP 165 AND 166: PHOTOGRAPHY JASON FRANK ROTHENBERG
PP 168–69: PHOTOGRAPHY HANUK

VIKTOR & ROLF
PP 170, 171 AND 174, BOTTOM RIGHT: MITCHELL SAMS
PP 172, 173 AND 174, LEFT AND TOP RIGHT: PETER STIGTER

VIVIENNE WESTWOOD
PP 176, 178, 180 AND 181: PHOTOGRAPHY CATWALKING.COM
P. 183: ANDREAS KRONTHALLER, LONDON, 2006, COURTESY
JUERGEN TELLER

WALTER VAN BEIRENDONCK
PP 182, 183, MIDDLE AND 184: PHOTOGRAPHY RONALD STOOPS
P. 183, LEFT: PHOTOGRAPHY KAREL FONTEYNE
P. 185: PHOTOGRAPHY PATRICK ROBIJN
P. 186: PHOTOGRAPHY J. B. MONDINO
P. 187: PHOTOGRAPHY F. DUMOULIN

WOODS & WOODS
PP 194, 196, 197 AND 199, TOP AND BOTTOM RIGHT:
PHOTOGRAPHY IVANHO HARLIM
P. 195: PHOTOGRAPHY IVANHO HARLIM, PUBLISHED IN
SUDDEUTSCHE ZEITUNG (GERMANY), ISSUE NO. 37, 2006
P. 199, TOP LEFT: PHOTOGRAPHY OLIVIER CLAISSE
FASHION SHOW MODEL CASTING BY JEAN MARC MASALA
AND WOODS & WOODS
VISUAL AND GRAPHIC ARTIST 2MANYDESIGNERS

YOHJI YAMAMOTO
PP 202 AND 205, TOP RIGHT: PHOTOGRAPHY MONICA FEUDI
P. 205, BOTTOM RIGHT: DRAWING YOHJI YAMAMOTO

DESIGNER CONTACTS

Aitor Throup *www.aitorthroup.com*

Alexander McQueen *www.alexandermcqueen.com*

Bernhard Willhelm *www.totemfashion.com*

Blaak *www.blaak.co.uk*

Burberry Prorsum *www.burberry.com*

Cosmic Wonder *www.cosmicwonder.com*

Costume National *www.costumenational.com*

D Squared2 *www.dsquared2.com*

Dior Homme *www.diorhomme.com*

Dries Van Noten *www.driesvannoten.be*

Duckie Brown *www.duckiebrown.com*

Frank Leder *www.frank-leder.com*

Gaspard Yurkievich *www.gaspardyurkievich.com*

Henrik Vibskov *www.henrikvibskov.com*

John Galliano *www.johngalliano.com*

Josep Abril *www.josepabril.com*

Kim Jones *www.kimjones.com*

Maison Martin Margiela *www.maisonmartinmargiela.com*

Marc Jacobs *www.marcjacobs.com*

Meadham/Kirchhoff *www.meadhamkirchhoff.com*

Patrik Söderstam *www.patriksoderstam.com*

Paul Smith *www.paulsmith.co.uk*

Peter Jensen *www.peterjensen.co.uk*

Raf Simons *www.rafsimons.com*

Rick Owens *www.owenscorp.com*

Siv Støldal *www.odd.at*

Spastor *www.spastor.org*

Stephan Schneider *www.stephanschneider.be*

Victor Glemaud *www.glemaud.com*

Viktor & Rolf *www.viktor-rolf.com*

Vivienne Westwood *www.viviennewestwood.co.uk*

Walter Van Beirendonck *www.waltervanbeirendonck.com*

Wendy & Jim *www.wujsympathisant.com*

Woods & Woods *www.woods-woods.com*

Yohji Yamamoto *www.yohjiyamamoto.co.jp*

ACKNOWLEDGMENTS

A huge thank you to all the designers, fashion houses and PRs for supporting this book. Many thanks to all the creatives who provided imagery, generously gave of their time for interviews and provided opportunities to witness their design practice.

Many thanks to everyone at Laurence King Publishing for backing this project, principally Helen Evans for allowing this book to evolve and notably John Jervis for sustaining the process. Thanks to Carol Franklin for meticulous copy-editing, Jay Hess for inspired art direction, Alicia Foley for persistent picture research and to project editor Catherine Hooper who excelled at a remarkable task and kept it all on track.

Special thanks to Dianne Roberts and Lee Widdows, both of whom have been inspirational figures and encouraged me from the beginning. A personal thanks to my parents for their incessant support, to Val Furphy for her alliance and especially to Jesper for keeping me sane.